Educating the Soul

Spiritual Healing and
Our Eternal Psychology™

Eric Thorton

EDUCATING THE SOUL : Spiritual Healing and Our Eternal Psychology™

Second Printing Published by

Eric Thorton Enterprises LLC
P.O. Box 1732
Woodinville, WA 98072

First Printing Published by

Red River Press, LA

First edition, first printing
First edition, second printing

ISBN: 978-0-615-22099-4

To my wife, Tsunami

Acknowledgments

Like any worthy story, mine has benefited from the invaluable contributions of other wonderful human beings: The other practitioners and professionals from whom I have learned so much: D.W. for teaching me to face my gifts; Armando Guzman for confirming what I let myself be a part of; Laura Smith, who showed me what was already there; Dan Lewis, Melynda MacIntosh, Richard Kiteaff, and a special thanks to Michael Hahn for confirming my sight; Sue Neufeld-Ellis for recognizing a very valuable aspect of this work and encouraging me on; my writing team, including Margaret Magwire, who taught me that it is okay to ask questions and helped me write the answers down and organize them. The Floating Gallery/Arbor Books, Joel and Andrew, and all that I have had the privilege to work with and learn from. To my friends who have waited so long to read this and have listened to the thoughts as they were given to me. To my editor, Lynn Gerlach, whose gift of language talent is nothing short of amazing, and, of course, to my family: my mother for being steadfast and encouraging and my children who are the greatest teachers one can have, but most importantly my wife, Tsunami, a woman of endless patience and understanding.

Contents

Chapters

Foreword

Editors don't generally write forewords for the books they edit. Editors usually confine their scribbling to such remarks as "Can you come up with a better example?" or "I'd move this to the conclusion," or simply "Huh??" This is a special book, though, and I have developed a special relationship with this author.

I first met Eric Thorton on paper two-and-half years ago when I had an opportunity to edit a very early draft of this book, sent to me by email through a third party. Along with my corrections and suggestions, I characterized this as a compelling, intriguing story, not only a great read, but capable of truly making a difference in people's lives. I thought it was one of the most important and unique manuscripts that had crossed my desk. I only wished I had some way to communicate that directly to the author.

For a year I watched for the book to hit the bookstores. Nothing. The manuscript haunted me. I went back and read it again, sure I had stumbled onto something very special. And there I found a little thread of hope: Eric Thorton's phone number!

It took a few days to work up the nerve to call him, but I had to know the fate of his book. He had no idea who I was when he answered the phone, but then he wouldn't have known about me, since we had worked through a third party. We had an animated discussion about his healing practice and writing efforts, but he told me he had no prospects for publishing at the time. He had begun to revise the manuscript, and I liked the things he was telling me about it. Then he asked me, "Uh, did you say you're an editor?" I said, "I'm your editor. I edited your manuscript." He told me he was currently in search of an editor, and we agreed without hesitation to work together.

Reading Eric's revised manuscript, I was more convinced than ever that this was a humble, truthful man with special gifts he wished to offer for the good of others. His story was as intriguing this time around as it had been in the past. And then I discovered Eric lived just a few miles from a close relative I visit several times a year! I vowed to meet him on my next family visit.

We agreed to meet at Starbucks. I suppose he was reluctant to bring a strange woman into his home, and I wasn't about to meet him anywhere but in a very public place. Would he be weird? Would he talk about my aura and hint that he could see into my soul or even my mind? Would he creep me out? Try "none of the above." Here was the guy next door, as he had described himself, just a friendly, affable guy with a good sense of humor—and the uncanny ability to help Spirit heal people who wish to be healed. After an hour of rapid-fire conversation, I knew I had to experience Eric's gifts firsthand. I asked for a healing session. He requested permission to contact my Guides through meditation to prepare himself for the session, which would be in a few days. He knew nothing of my medical history and preferred to keep it that way.

Now, I was not in any way ill or in pain or suffering. I simply wanted Eric to look inside me and tell me what he saw. After sharing with me what his meditation had revealed, various details of which confused either or both of us, I lay on a massage table, fully clothed, covered with a down comforter. (He had the windows open, and the weather was brisk.) Eric never touched me, never actually saw my body with his physical eyes. He consulted his Guide and mine, who apparently were stationed at the foot of the table. I neither saw them nor heard them.

Holding his hand about 10-12 inches above my body, he went where the Guides told him to go. Now, the session lasted four hours, and I won't bore you with all the details, many of which would be of interest to me only. But let me share a few of the surprising moments. When Eric's hand hovered over my liver, he suddenly asked, "Have you had chemotherapy?" Whoa! Indeed, I had undergone nine grueling months of chemotherapy 18 years prior. He said there were lingering traces of the drugs, which he would normally see in the kidneys, but the Guides wanted to remove them from my liver. "Go for it," was my answer. The room did not tremble; there was no great wind, no physical sensation at all. He did the job and moved on.

After several stops along the way, discussing the situation quietly and calmly with the Guides, Eric's hand made its way toward the site of my original tumor. Would he find it, I wondered. And, yes, when his hand hovered about 12 inches above the spot he said simply, "Oh, so this is where the cancer was." Bingo! He really could see into my body! Then he asked whether I had undergone radiation and, yes, I had. He said the Guides would like to remove the effects of the radiation, and, with my permission, he began making scooping motions in the air and sort of tossing aside something invisible. Suddenly he shook his hand at the wrist and grimaced. "Geez! How many treatments did you have?" I told him 30, and he shuddered and flicked his hand again, explaining that the effects of the radiation were scorching his palm. He turned to the invisible Guides (invisible to me, anyway) and asked very quietly, "Can you do something about this?" holding his palm out to them. After a few seconds he mumbled a "thanks" and continued removing the effects of the radiation.

The four-hour session was thorough and astounding, yet Eric remained matter-of-fact throughout. He never made any dramatic moves or spoke to the Guides in an affected voice. He did not become exhausted or weak. In fact, we kept up a friendly banter and even had a few laughs. I didn't go into a trance and he didn't speak in tongues or chant or do anything strange at all.

About a year later I returned for another healing session, again feeling fine but wanting to know what I could learn about myself. And I will go back again when I'm visiting in his area. Eric's ultimate goal is something he calls "education of the soul" through "Eternal Psychology™" As he explains in this book and on his web site, the physical body is the spirit's laboratory, the place where learning occurs through pain, discomfort and suffering. Only when we learn the root cause of the ailment do we truly grow from our illnesses, and only then can we achieve permanent healing. But the process goes beyond healing the physical body; it's about the progression of the soul for the purpose of improving and elevating the entire human species.

Eric Thorton has opened my mind to the possibility of exploring my purpose on earth, discovering the lessons I came here to learn and making progress in that learning. Now that he has shaken me to the core by surprising me with his knowledge of my being, I am determined to develop my own knowledge of my being and work on the education of my soul. Read the book; you'll probably want to do the same.

EDUCATING THE SOUL

Lynn Gerlach
Middleburg, Florida
December, 2007

Preface

I am a spiritual healer with uniquely developed gifts for moving energy to allow physical and emotional improvements in people's lives. Other than that, I am an ordinary man who works to support his family and pay his mortgage, worries about his expanding waistline, and eats, sleeps, laughs and cries just like anyone else.

In addition to my gifts as a medium and healer, I was granted another gift that seemed, for most of my life, more like a curse: I am dyslexic. For that reason, my knowledge of things spiritual and physical has come through hands-on experience, including trial and error, as well as through consulting with other practitioners. Academic research has never been my strong suit.

This is the story of a little boy who saw and felt things beyond the capabilities of other little children and grew to be a contractor who used his hands to build but only reluctantly to heal. My early life had its share of pain and loss, perhaps more than most. It also had more than its share of wondrous experiences involving amazing connections with other living creatures and incredible sources of energy and beauty. I assumed all little children saw and heard and felt these things. I was a little boy; what did I know?

When a client for whom I was doing some remodeling asked me, point blank, whether I was a healer, I nearly died of embarrassment. I was reluctant to admit to anyone that I could see into their energy, feel their pain, know their suffering. At the age of 29, I hadn't even told my loving wife (not that she didn't know). Dyslexic as I was, I had declined to read about spiritual healing or the other phenomena I had experienced. On the occasions I had been asked to participate in a healing session, I assumed the positive energy flowing through me was flowing through everyone else in the room too. As a child, as a man, what did I know?

Once I embraced my gifts, supported and assisted by an amazing psychotherapist to whom I had gone for career counseling, I began to build my healing practice and learn from a variety of excellent practitioners all around me. Experience taught me how to protect myself from danger, and my conscience taught me how to apply my gifts ethically for the good of humanity.

A few years ago, in agony with kidney stones to the point that I had to suspend my practice, I finally listened to the Guides on whom I had learned to rely for direction and leadership, and the message was clear: Write the book. For two years I stopped seeing patients in order to apply my overwhelmed dyslexic brain to the accomplishment of this writing task. My goals were pure and simple:

To bring to the general reading public, in the simplest of terms, an understanding of the process of spiritual healing.

To bring out into the sunlight the gift of healing which everyone possesses as a birthright, but which few of us develop and apply for the common good.

To open a dialog about the role of a healing tradition feared and shunned in contemporary society but rooted in every ancient tradition and revered in every culture throughout history.

To give hope to others who might recognize in themselves the signs of a special gift but who, like me, are confused about how or when or even whether it should be used.

My book is humble and unassuming, based on one man's experiences, with only meager mention of academic sources. My intention is not to pretend to know it all, but simply to share with the world that of which I am certain: That we are all united through the Absolute, no matter what we call that divine perfection; that we are each possessed of an immortal soul seeking to be educated and perfected; that our biological life on earth is a means of educating that soul for the ultimate uplifting of the entire human race; that some of us are more capable than others of facilitating the loving touch of the Absolute, through Spirit (the working hand of divine perfection), because we have gifts of sight and hearing, touch and healing more developed and accessible than the gifts of our fellow humans; that we are each tasked with using whatever gifts we have to improve our souls and so improve all of humanity.

This is my story; I hope it will start a conversation that moves spiritual healing into the cultural mainstream, offering encouragement and support for each individual 's exploration of his or her unique gifts.

In order to protect the privacy of those individuals with whom I have worked, all names, places and specific identifying data have been changed or deleted in the narrative that follows. Some information has been gathered from several healings and compressed into single stories for the purpose of clarity. All the facts and experiences of spiritual healing remain true, although any similarities to specific individuals or events are purely coincidental. The integrity of the emotional processes, spiritual and experiential data from my practice is completely maintained.

Introduction

This is the story of how I became a full-time spiritual healer and how I came to learn that healing could be used to enhance my personal life. I hope that, as you learn about my journey, you recognize how a new approach to healing can be incorporated into *your* life. Perhaps you will discover the keys to unlock your own joy and become more comfortable with this aspect of your own life. While each individual will discover his or her gifts in a unique way, I thought it would be useful and, I hope, interesting for others to learn how I awakened to my special gifts.

The mere mention of the phrase spiritual healing produces strong reactions from just about everyone, from the avowed skeptic to the true believer, the searcher to the cynic, and to those who think the concept is merely ridiculous. I fully appreciate all those reactions, having experienced each of them at various times myself. Tugging at my attention for some time has been an innate curiosity to know my own soul, and this curiosity has opened the door for my gifts of healing. My path has led me, at times reluctantly, to my current situation as a healer and medium. Here I stand today with an over-booked calendar of clients whom I've worked with on a wide variety of issues. My practice includes spiritual, psychological, emotional and physical healing, which, together, are recognized by the term etheric healing. Such healing is a process that awakens one's connection to the divine. My clients have received healing of broken bones, cancerous tumors, heart disease, blindness, hearing loss, and much more.

Spiritual healing does not preclude the use of modern medicine. (Sadly, a reciprocal attitude is hard to find.) Clients of spiritual healing have achieved what some have called miraculous results. This is not because I am a prophet or possess superhuman powers, but because, as a born healer, I have been able to foster a profound and very human connection with the Absolute for the purpose of healing. This is something we all can grow into; it is intrinsic to our human nature. The gift of spiritual healing is not a sixth sense, paranormal phenomenon, mysticism or any other unattainable concept that society has shrouded in mystery and set aside from mainstream culture. Such a connection to the divine is perfectly normal, although it does occur outside our current understanding of the laws of physics.

Think about it like this. Your brain is the control center, so your soul gives you information in the form of energy which stimulates a brain reaction much like the micro-currents used to stimulate the hearing centers of the brain to give a deaf person hearing. I cannot prove this scientifically, but the anecdotal evidence that such energy transference exists around our planet is undeniable. This occurs in our lives whether we are believers or skeptics. It includes the quiet knowings, the visions in the corner of our eyes, the greatest tool we all have and use every day. Why do we all turn and look when some stranger we've never met is pointing at the sky? This is because our souls are trying to preserve the somas (life) using our subconscious communication -- if something is falling on your head, you need to know, right? In those little ways, we all receive information from our souls. I am different simply because I have learned to pick up this tool and use it. The tool is communication with my soul, which is directly linked to all that we don't physically see, hear or access.

One of my objectives in writing this book is to dispel the mystery and misconceptions surrounding spiritual healing so people might open their minds to the myriad of possibilities beyond currently accepted attitudes. I wish to see them engage their own natural curiosity and abilities. Such a discovery can awaken the joy and peace we all seek throughout our lifetime.

As you read this book, maybe the question you will want to ask yourself is not, is this true or false? But rather, what if? What if this book begins to establish spiritual healing as a practical tool for use in your daily life, enabling you to understand and process the physical and emotional problems you have endured since birth? What if this book fosters a closer walk with that which we call divine? What if this book opens up new possibilities for conflict resolution? What if medical doctors would start to refer patients to healers?

I wish people could see and feel what I experience on a daily basis, because it could change the way they see themselves in the context of our world, as it changed me. I believe we would share a common reverence for life that reaches beyond a mother's womb and our nation's borders and could even make war obsolete.

This book is not intended as an academic work, but a compilation of cultural and practical knowledge. My intention is to open up a dialogue regarding the nature of spiritual healing (not just from my own limited point of view). I would like my readers to see how and why it works in people's lives and why it works. In order to illustrate that, I have used real-life examples from my own practice and that of psychotherapists with whom I have been working closely in the healing of mutual clients. Together we have seen how spiritual healing and the medium have dramatically affected a wide variety of clients.

True healing restores free will and brings balance to the somas, which is always for the higher good of the individual rather than what the individual might perceive he or she wants at that point in time.

Healing does not always unfold the way you expect, though, and that is why psychological processing is necessary to gain the full benefit of healing. At times the client needs outside help with this processing. Healing occurs on physical, emotional and spiritual levels, often in unusual combinations, but always for the education of our souls. We all have a body and a soul. The body's purpose is singular: to experience physical life for the soul. The body is finite and lineal. For a short period of time it is the vessel of learning for the soul. The body dies, but the soul keeps this knowledge forever. If we can look at the somas as the two different phenomena that they are, we might, just for a minute, get out of our own way, maybe even become less vested in our physical problems and find the joy that is there for us all.

I have seen many clients who failed to benefit from the full extent of their healing process because of their carefully guarded beliefs. Many people today have become complacent with the beliefs they have been taught. This complacency limits their capacity to be fully aware of their own abilities and birthright. It limits their view of how Spirit can and should be incorporated into all of our daily lives. This birthright is access to the vast sum of knowledge that can be engaged with the help of a spiritual healer/medium. When we exercise our spiritual free will, we expand beyond these limitations and open ourselves to the promise of complete healing. (By *spiritual free will* I mean a direct, intrinsic, uninfluenced connection with our own soul.) This is why spiritual free will plays an enormous role in individual healing. It allows each of us the individual freedom to learn and experience healing directly, without the constraints of man-made doctrines. If we go to the divine with a specific education, agenda or predisposition, we lose the lessons, much like starting kindergarten at the age of five with a Ph.D. The most valuable lessons of kindergarten would be lost to the already educated child. The most important lesson of school is to learn *how* to learn by oneself and with others. Paradigms created by previous knowledge block the experience.

It is important to understand that healing is not a New Age philosophy or cult and should not be mistaken for a religious doctrine, educational process or belief system. Consequently, this book is neither religious nor anti-religious in its message. The healing process I am talking about is neither heresy nor voodoo. And I do not claim to present here the entire story of spiritual healing. It is *my* story and *my* journey as a spiritual healer, a collaborative process that has brought together very dissimilar people in the creation of a practice synthesizing spiritual healing with psychotherapy. This is about an educational process, not a quick fix. I want to show you how spiritual healing, combined with psychological work, supports the overall progression of each individual's soul.

Healing has been documented in the earliest archeological finds around the world; it is referenced in our most ancient texts, yet is considered bogus by many in today's society. How and when did spiritual healing lose its legitimacy? When did we lose access to this powerful treatment method? Why are healers now seen as charlatans, and why is spiritual healing no longer embraced as an effective treatment for the body and soul? And why, despite the overwhelming pressure from society to discredit anything that can be seen or touched, do millions of people seek out healers, clairvoyants and other spiritual practitioners on a daily basis? We have an insatiable curiosity regarding the reality of Spirit, which underscores our intrinsic knowledge that the soul exists beyond the body. It almost seems as if the greater the resistance to this reality, the greater the intrinsic knowledge.

Healing is simple and clear. It is not sensational. It is a quiet knowing that fills our lives with peace and the understanding of our true purpose. It is the education of the soul, which brings us closer to that which we call divine. It is through this process of education that physical healing occurs. If physical healing occurs without the appreciation of the underlying cause, then the healing is not complete and the physical manifestations can return. It is like treating a backache with anti-inflammatory drugs. Sure, the pain will subside when the drugs take effect, but you have not addressed the cause of the backache. Is a joint out of alignment? Is it a problem with your posture? Is it caused by stress that manifests as muscular tension, which, in turn, pulls your spine out of alignment? Unless and until you address and resolve the underlying cause, the backache can return. True healing gets to the root cause of whatever ails you and, thus, can eliminate the problem permanently and completely.

Everyday life is not without its problems, and they take many forms, including physical and mental illness. Yet it is these very problems that are intended to provide the grist for our daily lives. The grist is the inherent dissatisfaction that keeps each of us searching even when we have found all the answers. It propels us to search until we find and embrace our intended spiritual purpose, often allowing for the uncovering of our spiritual gifts. It is because of this seeking process that we are not still living in caves. The soul education can appear arduous and painful to the physical body, and so it causes many people to take shortcuts, damaging the body-soul union and limiting their healing to one particular modality.

The tendency of the human physical body to take shortcuts can make us vulnerable to predatory or negative energy, which, in turn, has undermined our spiritual growth as a species. These shortcuts encompass everything from religion to science. If we separate the somas into the two basic parts, the body and soul, we might be able to distinguish the shortcuts the body wants from what is best for the soul. Keep in mind that what is ultimately best for the soul is ultimately best for the physical body too. We take a pill to get rid of the pain immediately instead of finding the meaning or metaphor of the pain in order to cure or heal permanently. We pray for an instant cure in a religious ceremony, revival or laying on of hands, and if we do not get what we want, we then legitimize with feelings of unworthiness, which is easier then finding why our prayers were not answered.

Remember, the soul seeks knowledge for its education. The body, on the other hand, the animal part of us, naturally seeks the immediate path of least resistance or the easy way out. When the shortcuts don't produce the desired results, we legitimize these failures on a personal level but also on civic and national levels in order to save face within our cultural parameters. These shortcuts can include: failing to seek mental health care because we are too proud, poor or smart; not seeking the help we need because it seems to have failed before; feeling too superior to seek help, and therefore relying on religious or scientific excuses. On civic levels, we shun new and different people entering our communities that come with different ideas. On the national level we tend to do the same thing by closing our cultural doors because of semantics and cultural differences. It is these rationalizations that form the foundations of our religious, socioeconomic and political myths.

It is my intention to begin to examine this phenomenon and how it affects our physical conditions and our learning processes. I will also attempt to explain how this predatory energy works, as well as why it is so effective. In doing so, many of the commonly believed myths regarding good and evil will be discussed, without the intention of debunking them, but rather, developing a language that is both straightforward and simple in order to discredit the false concepts holding our spiritual progression hostage.

I hope this book will be a vehicle to move healing into the mainstream of all cultures. In order to accomplish this, I make no judgments nor identify any one system or body of knowledge as the right one. And I certainly do not claim to have all the answers. Understanding of our purpose and potential is achieved through direct experience and cooperation. It is imperative to scrutinize the conflicts caused by physics, politics, religion, nationalism and economics. By examining these conflicts in a neutral, unbiased manner, we can begin to identify the impact they have had on our spiritual growth and see how they have been holding us in spiritual stagnation. I hope to encourage people to continue to do their own research and have ongoing dialogues to promote their souls' education.

My goal is to provide a view of our current spiritual climate that might explain why mankind is struggling with its spiritual evolution. Perhaps the discussion will open a new door for the dramatic spiritual growth intended for us all and provide a framework for understanding and reconnecting to our intrinsic wisdom. I also hope that people who have gifts whose potential they have not yet realized will read this book and begin to apply this knowledge to their own lives. Perhaps you, the reader, will see yourself in a different light and allow for the prospect that you, too, may be a spiritual healer in the rough.

Most of all, I want to bring spiritual healing out of the closet and place it squarely in the light of day, where it belongs. The fundamental truth regarding spiritual healing has been hidden away from us all, making it inaccessible as a tool to our joy. I aim to expose this legacy to the light of day so we can all enjoy the beauty and love of spiritual healing.

Chapter One: My Greatest Fears

Sitting in my easy chair watching my three children playing in our yard, I try to cope with the fear welling up inside me. What have I done? Where will this book take me? Tears come to my eyes as I think back over my life and wonder at all the amazing experiences that have brought me to this moment. Will my fear of losing my anonymity be unfounded, or will the consequences of publishing my thoughts and experiences be even worse than I can envision? I have never had a desire to be famous. I prefer to live a quiet and peaceful life with my family. What will publication of a book do to them? Is the response to my unusual calling going to make my worst fear -- of being misunderstood -- come true?

Until fairly recently I had been a self-employed contractor, a career I had enjoyed for about twenty years. I was always able to provide for my growing family and took great pleasure in my work, particularly in the interactions with my clientele. For me, the key to a successful business was always good communication and understanding. In the course of working on lengthy or multiple projects, I often came to know my clients well. In fact, my wife would regularly remark how I was part remodeler and part counselor. The phone would frequently ring during and after dinner with clients calling to say hello. I would find myself in conversations about their worries and concerns that had nothing to do with remodeling and were more about their issues than about what needed fixing. My wife often referred to me as the man with two tool bags, one for listening and one for repairs. It did not seem unusual to me that they would seek me out for a sympathetic ear. In some cases I became like an extended family member and was asked to attend family gatherings and even funerals.

The work as a contractor was tough because of the long hours of physical labor, but it was satisfying, as I got to see tangible results. There is no feeling that can compare to having built something with your own two hands and knowing that you helped someone live a better life. No drama, just parts and a sympathetic ear. Looking back on this time in my life, I can see how my natural healing gifts were emerging, even within the context of general contracting.

Over the years, I did several repair or remodeling jobs for one particular local couple. While working on their beach cabin, which had fallen into extreme disrepair, I experienced a phenomenon that I will call, for now, a knowing. It ultimately helped me save the cabin from total ruin. In truth, this cabin should have been torn down, but the local building codes prevented any new construction on the site. I knew the structure was riddled with powder post beetles, a highly destructive insect that turns wood into powder. These beetles had eaten away all the structural framing, which meant I had to replace all four sides of the cabin, one at a time, to prevent a total collapse. As I was tearing down the north wall, I began to receive mental images of the cabin leaning. They were like the thoughts you have just before sleep, when the visual part of your brain begins to gear up in anticipation of the dreams to come. These images became stronger when I ignored them, until I was finally driven to get a 30-foot beam to brace the cabin. As I tightened the brace, I noticed the entire structure shifting into alignment. That night, we had a storm that surely would have blown the cabin down were it not for the support I had installed. I thanked God that I responded to those startling images which have now proven to be extremely useful in my work.

During the four-month period I worked on this cabin, I noticed that the owner was becoming seriously ill, though he was apparently unaware of it. I noticed his joyful demeanor slipping away, and I saw him come home overly exhausted at the end of each day. Still, I knew I had to keep this knowledge to myself. Every time I laid eyes on this man, I actually *saw* deterioration of his tissues. He had become a friend over the years, and to see this happening to him was painful. My preoccupation built up to the point that, in a moment of complete distraction, I actually drove my truck into a sand pile on the job site. It was then that I knew I had to share with someone what I was seeing.

I risked telling my wife. In our five years of marriage, I had never mentioned to her my ability to see illness. My heart raced and my stomach churned as I began to utter the story. I had no idea how she would react, so I started out slowly. I remember her sitting at our old, white, Formica kitchen table with chain-sawn legs, a relic my great uncle had built for my grandfather. As she listened to my story, her expression was a mix of sadness and insight. She was not surprised by what I was telling her; it was as if she had known all along. Her understanding meant a lot to me because, even today, I sometimes feel terribly alone in these gifts. Her continued support has been a mainstay in my life.

As a result of the discussion, we agreed that I should continue to keep this knowledge to myself. After all, what would my client think if I walked up to him and said, "Hey, I just thought I should let you know that you are ill. I know you don't feel it, but I can see it. Don't ask me how. I just can." What would you think if your building contractor said that to you? Would you look at the messenger in total disbelief? What would my subcontractors have thought, had they heard such remarks from me? I would have been a laughingstock. Even worse, would I be responsible for totally redirecting this person from his life journey?

I now know that being a good steward of healing gifts requires that I follow divine guidance regarding when and how to speak of these *knowings*. To do otherwise, I would be acting as a god, and my gifts would stagnate, diminish, or disappear altogether. It is not up to me to tell somebody something just because I can. It is never the seer's job to influence anyone's personal experience unless asked to do so by that person, operating within their own free will. This is a mistake I have witnessed many healers and seers make. They justify their actions out of ego and ignorance, when truly this indicates that their own gifts are not fully matured.

I continued with the jobs this couple gave me, making no mention of what I saw. Again, this was difficult for me, as we were also friends. About two years after I first noticed the man's illness, I found out he had been diagnosed with terminal cancer. One day, while I was working on another job for them, his wife approached me and asked, "Are you a healer?" I was stunned at her timing. All my subcontractors were standing around, and I didn't want them to think I was strange, so I just quietly said to her, "Call me later." I was surprised that she had asked me out of the blue, but not surprised by the question. To be honest, I had been expecting for some time that something like this would happen. Nothing could prepare me, however, for the challenge that lay ahead or the chain of events that would lead me to where I am today.

As young as the age of five or six I had started noticing a wonderful feeling whenever I talked about God or Jesus or the Holy Spirit. (I use these terms because my mother raised me in the Catholic Church, much to my father's chagrin. For each of us, our vocabulary is based on the frame of reference we were given as a child.) I'm referring to a feeling of warmth that would come into my heart, not unlike that safe, enveloping hug a child craves from a loving parent. This feeling was particularly strong when someone in need was near me. I would experience this physical knowing and then, suddenly, a slight shift within occurred and I would feel the person's physical and/or emotional pain. I did not know why they were under duress; I just felt it. I became very compassionate, in the literal sense, experiencing tremendous empathy for people in need, and also a great desire to alleviate their suffering. I never talked about this because it was a normal occurrence for me. After all, as a child, everything you experience firsthand is "normal," even routine, until you are told otherwise.

One such experience occurred when I was about thirteen. During a First Communion church service, my attention was drawn to a particular little girl walking down the aisle in her white dress. I was overcome with a deep, confused sadness that suddenly convinced me I had to be perfect or I would be punished. My compassion was drawn to her. Our eyes met and, as they did, I was shown her pain and sorrow. I saw the damaging incidents that had filled her life up to that point. My attention was also drawn to her parents, who were attending the service.

15

I was filled with dread at the sight of them because I could feel their daughter's powerlessness in their presence. Clearly, they were the cause of her pain. Many years later, this little girl, now a grown woman, came back into my life, and the truth of my early experience was confirmed by her own recounting of her childhood. As she told me her story, I relived what I had seen at the age of thirteen. Without realizing it, she confirmed for me one of my earliest experiences as a seer with a desire to heal. I never let her know what I had been shown so many years before, and I now realize it was all for my education, to teach me compassion for the human condition.

These experiences of intense insight also occurred with plants and animals. Gradually I became aware of my ability to sense the energy of plants and animals. I could understand their needs and wants without any outward signs of communication. I would respond to what I "just knew" they wanted, and they responded to me. Everyone said I had a green thumb, but the fact was I *knew* what the plants needed. Animals that would not let anyone else come near would let me near them.

When I was young, the neighbors had a collie that befriended me. The dog's owner was abusive and liked to brag about killing animals for no reason. This man enjoyed shooting animals or finding other means to kill them. His collie would find me in my yard and spend hours playing and hanging out with me. When his owner returned home, the dog would become skittish and run off and hide. The collie was always calm with me and always very nervous with his owner. I felt the dog knew his human was an animal killer and would kill him on a whim. Even at my young age, I had a *knowing* that the collie sensed he wasn't safe with his owner. Sadly, one particularly noisy Fourth of July, the dog ran away, never to be heard from again. No doubt he thought the fireworks were the sounds of his owner's gun threatening his life.

One of the most profound incidents of my childhood took place when I was eight and my little brother Roger was five. My mother and stepfather owned a marina on a lake. It was a working marina with a gas dock, boatlift and living quarters above a boat repair shop. There were apartments overlooking the marina, with year-round activity. The marina had four docks, one of which was elevated above the high water line for fuel pump safety. I learned to work here. I begged for jobs because I wanted to learn about boats and how they went together. I earned 25 cents an hour for doing odd jobs. I liked working with my stepfather because he was kind and patient with me. We all learned to water ski and "sail" boats. In fact, my stepfather actually built me a five-foot sailboat so I could sail about the marina on my own. What great fun! I felt so special to have my own real boat. Don't get me wrong: Both parents were very concerned about safety. We always had our life jackets on if we were near the water.

Well, my little brother Roger and I were buddies, even though he was three years younger. He was an active spirit, and I was always chasing after him. We had many games of hide-n-seek, and we shared everything we could: toys, games and secrets. I helped with him all I could when he was a baby, so he knew me well; I had been at his side since his birth. One late winter morning at the marina, my mother and new stepfather had stepped out to get some lunch for the family, leaving my older stepbrothers in charge. Roger ran out of the marina living quarters to hide from me, as he did frequently during our games of hide-and-seek. My mother and stepfather were very strict about our wearing life vests around the marina, and I had taken the time to put mine on. Roger had not… and he was ahead of me.

I went out looking for Roger, walking the entire length of each floating wooden dock and checking in each boat as I went. I remember a sense of dread creeping into me. Even though I was freezing, I checked each dock and boat twice. Slowly, like poison seeping into my veins, I began to feel desperation. Where was Roger? It hadn't occurred to me to look in the water. Terror set in as I continued to come up empty in my search. I could usually find Roger easily. I was beginning to panic when I noticed my coat and hat in the dark water off the main service dock. I immediately started screaming, and I remember seeing a man in a dive suit calling down to me from the fourth floor.

"What's wrong?"

I yelled back at him that I saw my hat and coat in the lake and that my brother was missing. The next thing I knew he was rushing toward me in full dive gear. The diver jumped into the lake where my hat and coat were just as my mother came over the hill. Her pain was just beginning; soon her worst fears would be realized. With a jolt to my heart, I comprehended that my little brother was gone. My gift of compassion felt more like a curse at that moment because I was also feeling my mother's anguish as if it were my own. I remember her husband holding her back from jumping in the lake. "It's too late," echoed through the marina. (I can now fully appreciate her pain because I have children of my own.)

As I stood at the lake's edge, police divers, news reporters and camera crews began to line the docks. I remember ambulances, crowds of people and lots of yelling, yet I felt completely alone and detached. I continued to scan the boats, thinking Roger must be hiding, and then I heard someone yell, "We found the body!" What had taken three hours seemed an eternity. I'll never forget the image of the divers hoisting Roger's limp, lifeless body out of the cold waters. At the time, it didn't seem odd that I was watching all the commotion from the small dock to the east of the main service dock. From where I was standing, I could see a beautiful smile on my brother's face as the divers lifted his body from the freezing lake. I remember seeing the large, red bump on his forehead, which must have happened when he fell from the finger dock, hitting his head on the empty boat hull next to where I found my coat and hat floating in the water. I remember feeling eerily calm and isolated from where I stood, but somehow I knew this was the place I needed to be.

The tragedy did not stop with my brother's untimely death. That night, my biological father found out about the accident and came out of the mountains. He was intent on stealing the body and taking it to a private graveyard somewhere in the Cascades and taking my two older blood brothers and me with him into the mountains, and he was prepared to kill my mother, my stepfather and anyone else who might get in his way. As he exploded into the living room of our house, he picked up my 225-pound grandfather and tossed him through the air like a twig. He took his German Lugar pistol from his pants and attacked my stepfather and my mother. Neighbors seized my brothers and me and hurried us from the house, over fences and through bushes to the safety of a neighbor's house. Can you imagine my mother, distraught at the loss of her child, now having to deal with a maniac intent on hurting her and taking her other children? Fortunately, no one got shot, but my mother and stepfather were in the hospital for a week, both injured physically and in the throes of an emotional breakdown.

Watching the news the next day, I was astounded to see myself standing next to my mother on the main service dock as divers pulled my little brother's body from the water. Mother was sobbing as she shielded me from the gruesome sight of the body. I noticed that I had my eyes closed and was turned away from the scene. I have absolutely no recollection of it happening like that, even though I had the evidence in front of me. I clearly remember seeing the entire event from my vantage point on the next dock.

I was only eight years old and not quite sure what to make of my experience, so it remained a persistent question tucked in the back of my mind. From time to time, I would find myself thinking about the beautiful smile on Roger's face. I thought about the peace I had seen radiating from his body as a pure white light, and I knew he was happy. Looking back on it now, I can see that the trauma of the event plunged me into a state of shock, and it was only the lovely smile I had seen on Roger's face that kept me from becoming totally despondent.

My recollection of the events of Roger's death kept haunting me. How could I have been in one place and yet have a memory of the tragedy from a totally different position? As I matured, I began to understand that dead bodies don't smile, nor do they glow. I realized that I had received a "gift" from Roger and the Holy Spirit. The gift was the peace I needed to make it through the tragedy, as well as a realization or awakening of something inside me that could not be denied: the gift of seeing and the gift of knowledge. It also gave me my first realization that the body is separate from the soul. I believe that part of the purpose of my brother's life was to help awaken my gifts. This was not his only purpose, by any means, but it was one of his life's greatest gifts to me. Looking back on the incident today, I can only imagine that what happened was an out-of-body experience and a very real, intuitive communication between Roger and me. It was as if Roger was speaking directly to me.

It seemed to me that almost as soon as one such experience was over, another would occur. Each experience made me more comfortable with who I was meant to be. This was a completely unconscious process that unfolded naturally in my life, just as growth and maturity happen to all children, incrementally and sometimes imperceptibly. I never felt afraid of these happenings because they always made me feel safe. I didn't think of these experiences or myself as unusual, as they were all very genuine. I never asked for anything; it just happened.

Another one of these experiences came to me when I was about ten years old. My friend Ryan and I were in the backyard. We had made a dirt pile and were playing king of the mountain. In the midst of our shoving and pushing, he fell over and began to cry. I couldn't figure this out because he wasn't really hurt. He wouldn't stop crying, so I asked him what the problem was. He blurted out, "I have cancer!" After he wiped the dirt and tears off his face, he told me he had to go to the hospital to have an operation. He was visibly scared. He told me he had waited a long time to tell his mom about a pain he had been having, and, when he did, she immediately took him to their family doctor. This really freaked him out because he could see that his mom and the doctor were upset. Ryan had to go to another doctor who had taken X-rays and even taken some of his tissue for tests. That's when he found out it was cancer. Ryan needed emergency surgery if he were to have any chance at all of survival.

Ryan's mother was terrified. She called the local parish priest, who put her in touch with a Dominican nun known for her prayers of intercession (asking for God to change an outcome). The Dominican sister was living in another state at the time, but she arranged for the whole family to gather around Ryan in a prayer circle the day before the operation. Ryan's mother asked me to be a part of this prayer session. I agreed without really giving it a second thought because it seemed like a normal thing to do. (Looking back on her inclusion of me in this private family matter, I can only guess that she must have sensed something about me.)

I went to Ryan's house, not knowing what to expect. The nun was already on the phone, and she asked us all to huddle around Ryan in a circle. I found myself in this huddle with Ryan's family, my hand on my friend's shoulder, with the rest of the family touching Ryan also. Ryan's mom was on his other side, completing the prayer circle. The nun opened with a prayer of petition for God's will to be done. At that same moment I felt warmth envelop me and flow down my right arm, into my hand as it rested on Ryan's shoulder. I felt a weight pressing down on my shoulders as a wonderful flush of energy unleashed itself around me. I felt it come over my head, along my arm and out over my right hand. What a joyful moment! It felt so normal and natural that it never occurred to me everyone else wasn't experiencing the same thing. The energy running about me brought tears of peace, because even at that young age, I knew this energy was from God. I wondered at the time if anyone noticed my eyes well up with tears or my body shake slightly.

The next day, Ryan went into surgery early in the morning. The physicians were prepared to take out all the cancerous tissue seen on the X-ray, as well as anything else affected by the malignancy. Ryan was already scheduled for radiation treatment and chemotherapy, following the surgery, to make sure all the cancer cells were killed. However, when the surgeons opened him up, they discovered the cancer had "spontaneously disappeared." There were no signs of the malignancy noted in the previous biopsy, so he was never sent for radiation or chemotherapy. We were all overjoyed. The relief to his family spread through the neighborhood. For me, it had all unfolded just the way it was supposed to. I thanked God for the blessing, just as I would for anything else in my life. It never occurred to me that this was some great feat. To me, it was simply the way God worked. Nothing more was ever said about the prayer circle or the subsequent "miracle." Ryan is still alive and healthy, happily married and doing well. Now, 34 years later, he has had no recurrence of the cancer.

Looking back, I recognize that this was the first time I was used in a conscious manner to let the healing power of the Holy Spirit come over me and affect another person. I still remember that peaceful feeling of the energy coming forth and enveloping my friend and me.

This event was a powerful reaffirmation of God's presence in my life. It also occurs to me now that this is the way all of us are supposed to experience the Absolute – directly, with no intermediary, innocently, and with no expectation and no fear.

Around this same time, I started noticing the presence of something around me, a sort of glow. It looked like the multi-colored rainbow effect you can see in the fine mist of a sprinkler. Slowly, I began to notice this beautiful glow around others and soon came to realize I could see it around everyone. We each have a unique aura, which is as individual as a snowflake or a fingerprint. In these early stages of seeing, I often had to blink in order to see the actual person. In other words, I had to learn how to use this gift of sight correctly so it would not interfere with my physical life experience. Auras vary in shade and substance. Some auras are dull, as if they are overshadowed. These I found repulsive and today I know I was seeing "polluted energy." The darker the area, the more it attracted my attention. Dark areas would make me agitated or draw my compassion, depending on what energy was emanating from them. I began to notice a pattern with people who were sick or troubled or both. I had not yet put all the pieces together and did not realize this was a gift; however, I was becoming more aware of these occurrences in my life. I was also becoming much more empathetic to all of God's creation, because I could see the life force.

My ability to sense this type of energy was not limited to people, and I began to notice auras around animals, trees and everything else. Because of this discovery I had a sense that the Absolute worked in many ways and was to be found not only in church but also in all things and all people. This was especially real for me during a trip with friends through northern California. I was eleven years old and excited to be visiting this part of California for the first time.

My friends' parents drove us down in a battered old station wagon that looked as if it wasn't up to the trip, but, as kids, we were oblivious to such things and enjoyed being on an adventure. We made a stop at the coastal redwood forests along the way, and I recall looking from the car window, amazed by the beauty of these ancient giants. I was sure I could feel something from the trees. As I became aware of the magnificent energy emanating from them, I noticed a wisdom and purity much like that which emanates from a giant blue whale.

I stepped out of the car at the site of the cathedral trees and the Paul Bunyan and Seven Dwarves exhibit and almost fainted from this pure, innocent source of energy that completely enveloped me. It was as if the energy looked at us and gave each one of us exactly what we needed at that moment in time. It gave me joy that nearly overwhelmed me. It caused me to take in so much oxygen that I hyperventilated. The energy seemed to be pure love. I had never before experienced the untainted energy of God's creation. My body began to tremble as I awakened to the reality of this magnificent, life-giving force. I felt more alive here than I had since before Roger's death. My heart beat so fast it felt like it was going to burst through my chest. I wanted to run and jump and laugh out loud. I saw life moving and vibrating in every corner of my field of vision. This all happened instantaneously. I was overjoyed by the scent of the forest and the change this energy made in my aura as well as in the auras of most of the other people I saw there. Unfortunately, no one else in my group seemed to register any of this. In fact, my friends were oblivious to everything except their squabbling, and, of course, their parents were aware only of this distraction. In this setting, it was as if I was in my own world, unattached to my friends. Sadly, we stayed there for just a few hours. I longed to be able to stay there forever.

As we left, we drove along a peaceful, paved road with huge trees on either side. I felt as though we were leaving a great cathedral of God's creation, and the feelings that stirred deep within my soul were screaming out for me to remain there. "No. Don't leave. You will never have this chance again!" Tears welled up in my eyes in a very private moment, sitting in the front passenger seat of the car, as I felt that life force ebb away from my heart. This childhood experience left a profound impression on me of the greatness of God's garden and gave me the knowledge that a truly holy place was to be found on the coast of California. And it gave me great hope. I now know we all require the energy of creation to nurture and balance our bodies.

At such a young age, I could not yet fully appreciate the greatness of this life force, nor how fleeting it would be due to man's encroachment. As an adult, I have gone back to visit the trees only to experience a great sadness and emptiness caused by our ruthless harvesting of their magnificent timber. I wanted to embrace them and give them the joy they had once given me. I cried, and still do, for their plight and their pain. To this day, the conflict this causes within me leaves me sad and awestruck at the same time. I can still see the magnificent abundance of life in those forests as if it were yesterday, and, at the same time I'm aware of the ruin now left behind in man's wake. I don't believe these same energies of life are found anywhere else in this world, and it will be a sad day when these trees are lost forever.

When school started that fall, I started at a new private Catholic school in Washington State. It was an eventful year because I began to realize that my experience in the redwoods forest showed me life could go on in the wake of my brother's death. I started playing soccer at school and found myself able to joke around with my new classmates. I began to open up to life and allow myself to participate. Part of this process was becoming more open with people and being more aware of their feelings. I felt safe enough not to need to shut myself off from others.

I remember an incident during this time with my religious education teacher. She was a meek individual, not good at controlling her class, which was scheduled right after lunch. We were a rowdy bunch, and when she left us unattended for a few moments, a food fight broke out. Our teacher was not equipped to deal with such unruly behavior, and when she came into the class and saw the mess and commotion, she was not able to stop the chaos. In frustration, the teacher burst into tears and ran out of the room. I just sat there and died a little as feelings of guilt washed over me. Being able to feel the teacher's pain overwhelmed me. I froze in the anguish we had caused. My heart went out to her and, at that very moment, I experienced physical pain and redness in my hands, feet and my left side. I did not realize at the time that I was experiencing what is called stigmata. I experience this anytime I am holding back or resisting expression of the Holy Spirit. My heart had gone out to my teacher, and because my compassion had no outlet at that moment, I developed these red marks.

Stigmata are recognized as the manifestations of the wounds suffered by Christ during the crucifixion. Sometimes, when the stigmata were mentioned during discussions at church, the signs would appear on my body, although they were minor, much like a rash. I could not comprehend the concept. It made no sense to me that Christ would want anyone to suffer with His physical wounds. After all, His ministry was one of compassion, not pain. These manifestations would usually subside shortly afterward, but I remember one time in particular that the pain was so bad that I nearly asked for help. I did not want to draw attention to myself, however, so I decided to suffer through it. If it had been a cut or a bruise I would certainly have asked for help, but since it was something I could not explain, and since we were taught stigmata appeared only on "saints," I kept my mouth shut.

A few weeks later, in the same religious education class, we were given this assignment: "Write down the most significant event of your life and what you learned from it." I felt close enough to this teacher to risk being honest, because I knew she felt great pain and compassion for people. For the first time since Roger died, I allowed myself to go back over the events of his death and reflect on what I could possibly have learned from such a tragedy. I wrote: "My little brother Roger drowned at the family marina. I learned never to be too close to anybody because they could die and cause you pain."

The teacher took me aside after reading my paper and sympathized with me as best she could. Her compassion in that moment helped me go forward in life until I was ready to explore more of my issues regarding Roger's death.

My next "defining" moment came a few months later. All eighth-graders are of age for "confirmation," a rite of passage in the Catholic Church in which we were supposed to confirm our faith in the "one and only Church of God," now that we were supposedly old enough to make such decisions for ourselves. All "good Catholic" children were expected to go through this ritual, which was eagerly anticipated by their families. During the preparations for the ceremony, we were impressed with the seriousness of the commitment we were about to make. All of our parents would be there, as well as the bishop of the archdiocese. Everyone would expect us to be the next generation of Catholics and carry on the traditions of the "only way to God."

By this time, I could "see" whether or not the Holy Spirit was present in the church or its sacraments. When it came time for me to sign the document of confirmation, I could not do so in good conscience. The principal called me to her office in an attempt to badger me into participating in the confirmation process. When I refused, she called my mother, who, thankfully, stood behind my convictions. This infuriated the principal, who lectured me on the seriousness of this decision and threatened that I would burn in hell if I did not go through with the sacrament. I tried to explain my position, but that did not matter to her. Only my soul mattered, she informed me.

We all sat together as a class during the ceremony, and, when it was our turn, I was forced to sit alone in the pew while all my classmates filed before the bishop to kiss his ring. I never did sign the document. At the age of twelve, I knew far more truth existed than the doctrine of one church. I had seen God in churches as well as in the forest and the trees. I could see and feel the presence of God in people of all creeds and nationalities and from all walks of life.

One night, I was surprised and seriously frightened by the noise of a fight between two animals in the backyard of our family home. It went on for some time, and I could sense a high level of desperation and pain in one of the animals. The next morning, I went outside to enjoy the sunshine and check the area for evidence of the skirmish. When I approached the area where I thought the scuffle had occurred, I heard an unusual noise. It was a strange, low, growling sound coming from a pile of wood waiting to be built into a garage. Suddenly, the sight of a mother bobcat and her young startled me. The mother had obviously been hurt, as there was blood on the fur on the back of her neck and down her right side, but she was still trying to move her litter from place to place to protect them. I froze with fear, afraid to breathe, having been told these were desperate, vicious animals.

Out of character for a mother protecting her young, she looked at me with curiosity instead of fear. She came closer and stopped about ten feet away from me. My panic was rising when I began to feel that wonderful, warm feeling from the Holy Spirit flood over me. As I watched the mother bobcat, she seemed to relax and I "saw" how she had been wounded. At that precise moment I was shown the fight I had heard the night before. It was between her and some raccoons that were after her young. She had defended her kittens bravely, but at grave consequence to herself. I knew she was fatally wounded. I watched in amazement as the energy from around me seemed to radiate out to the animal. It was as if we were both engulfed in a sparkling white light. The bobcat appeared to become sleepy and, right before my eyes, her fur smoothed out and the blood disappeared. It was like time-lapse photography. Her body just seemed to renew itself. This went on for about five minutes, and then it was all over.

The white, sparkling energy subsided and the bobcat came out of her daze and ran back to the young she had so fiercely protected. She pulled out her four kittens in broad daylight and moved them to a new location. As she was moving her last kitten, she looked back at me and lowered her head and blinked slowly, much like a domestic cat would do. It was as if she were saying thank you. I could feel her gratitude. I never saw that animal again, nor any other bobcat in our area. I remember being at ease with what happened, yet at the same time keenly aware of how remarkable it was. But I still didn't think these incidents were unique to me. I wondered what other people thought about this type of thing when it happened to them.

My young life was filled with incidents like this, which I kept to myself in part because of an underlying reticence which I now know was a subconscious protective tool. In my heart I believed all people were capable of sensing the energy of trees and animals and the life force in all things. I did not feel unique because of my abilities and, looking back, I never thought of myself as having special gifts.

By age 29, however, I was becoming aware of the uncommon nature of these occurrences, which is why I didn't respond directly to my client's question regarding whether or not I was a healer. To be honest, I felt mortified to discuss something like that in front of my subcontractors because I didn't want to be seen as a freak. All my life I had held mainstream attitudes about anything beyond the five senses, and now I was being confronted with my own truth in front of a lot of other mainstream thinkers. Was I a freak after all? My gut reaction stopped me in my tracks. This was not a simple moment for me. This woman, June, had no idea of the deep struggle taking place inside me.

When I spoke with June later that day she sounded overwhelmed with sadness. "Rick is already in hospice at Lanier," she told me.

I could hear the pain in her voice as she tried to say this quietly because her small children were playing in the background. June quietly continued, "The cancer is riddling his body and the illness is incurable at this stage." I could only imagine how utterly devastating this must have been for her. It was all the more upsetting for me because I had seen his illness progressing for several years. This is part of the burden of being a seer and something that requires innocence and boundaries. By that I mean that the healer must maintain respect for people's own life experiences.

I got the sense this was the first time June had verbalized the seriousness of her husband's condition. Her pain permeated her every word as she told me he was not expected to live for more than two weeks. A wave of sympathy flooded over me. I could feel her anguish. It struck me very hard because I had known death at such a young age, and I realized how difficult it would be for her young, innocent children to make sense of this. So I risked my deepest secret. This pain that sat in the deepest part of my conscience urged me to reassure her that I had been used for healing many times before, but I hedged the words and finished the line with "I do not consider myself a healer." The truth was, I was a contractor by profession and didn't really know what to do to help her husband. I did tell her that I knew someone who was a prayer healer and that I would be happy to talk to her on her husband's behalf. She gratefully accepted my offer, so I called our family friend, Sister Sara.

When I had Sister Sara on the phone, she told me she had the gift of prayer, not of healing. She helped me understand the difference between a healer and someone with the gift of prayer. She defined a true spiritual healer as someone with the gift of command. She made the distinction between spiritual healing and the gift of "pleading" or prayer. When Sister Sara is praying, she is petitioning "God" for something to be done on behalf of another. Because it is ultimately the "will of God" that is being petitioned, the answer to the prayer is unknown. Sister Sara said it is as if a child is asking a parent for something out of the ordinary, in essence, a miracle. A child may ask for many things without the full understanding of whether or not it is in her best interests. In this case, June is asking for a cure of her husband's cancer without knowing whether this is part of his larger life plan. Sister Sara told me of a few incidents in which her prayers had been answered. She also told me about a healer with whom she used to pray, another nun in California. She had worked with this nun before, but the woman had recently passed away. I immediately thought to myself, "Oh, no. What am I going to tell June?" Sister Sara then said something to me, which I will never forget.

"Eric, you are a healer," she said. "You have the gift of command. I can pray with you for your friend; however, you need to be there in order to bring the energy of the Holy Spirit directly to this man."

Her words shook me to the core. The idea of standing in front of people who knew me as a contractor and acting as a spiritual healer, trusting God to be there no matter what, was, frankly, terrifying. To have the audacity to even think that God would show up seemed utterly impossible. Who was I to command the power of the Holy Spirit? Damn near panic set in. I don't know why I agreed to try; perhaps it was because I promised June I would help, and I could not turn away from friends in need.

We all agreed on a time to meet at the hospice. June was extremely grateful but doubtful that her husband, an ex-Catholic, would agree to our help. A week later, she called me back and told me her husband had just had an operation on his spine to remove a tumor that had left him unable to walk. Things did not look good. He was dying as we spoke, and he was now prepared to try anything. It made me feel he was trivializing our help.

The next day, June, Sister Sara and I went to the hospice center at Lanier. Sister Sara asked June's husband, Rick, a few questions about healing and the Holy Spirit, which he answered skeptically. In fact, he trivialized the existence of God in general, and only the day before had refused to allow a priest to anoint him. As an ex-Catholic, he had only bad memories of the Church that had tainted his experience of God. Rick all but turned us away; however, he settled down when his wife pleaded with him to let us continue.

Sister Sara asked Rick if I could lay my hands on him. I panicked again but kept it to myself. To touch another human being in the name of God! What would I do? What would I say? What would happen? He agreed, saying that he trusted me. We had known each other for years, and he figured it couldn't hurt. So I punted -- I put one hand on his shoulder and the other on his chest, very lightly.

Sister Sara went to the side of his bed and began to pray in tongues, which made me uncomfortable. I could only imagine Rick's eyes rolling in his head as this unfolded. I felt nothing at first. Then, suddenly, I felt warmth and a weight envelop me. I began to tremble as this energy moved around me, down my arms and over my hands. I watched the energy flow into Rick's body wherever I placed my hands. His wife began to sob uncontrollably, and Sister Sara prayed louder. Powered by a force greater than mine, my hands began to move over areas of his body, stop for a moment and spontaneously move to another area. Throughout this time I was shaking and sweating. I was a wreck and felt physically drained. After what seemed like an hour, I could no longer stand up. In what must have appeared to be a rather dramatic moment, I had to toss myself away from Rick and collapse into a chair. (Things have changed a bit since then, and I no longer have such a drastic reaction when healing people.)

Sister Sara almost pounced on Rick in her eagerness to question him about what he had felt. He said he felt peace and some warmth, but seemed more concerned with the fact that I looked terrible. I felt terrible, too. I could feel his cancer and his pain. It was awful. I had no drugs to dull it and I could hardly bear the agony. Sister Sara very quickly said our good-byes and rushed all of us out of the room.

On the way out, Sister Sara said she needed to pray to release the energy I had apparently absorbed from Rick. About halfway to the car, she uttered the prayer of release and, suddenly, all three of us were lifted into the air and thrown to the ground. At first, we were scared

(Wouldn't you be?), then dumbfounded as we noticed our scraped knees and elbows and our glasses, which had been thrown to one side. June began to cry, and I was immediately concerned about both of them. I knew Sister Sara, at 73, was in no condition for such physical abuse. As we picked ourselves up, she tried to explain what had happened. She said that I had taken on whatever made Rick sick, and that he would be fine now, and so would I. She informed me that I would be sore for a number of days. I have to admit, at that time I was as skeptical as Rick, but I was sore for about ten days, just as had been predicted.

About six weeks later, I heard from one of Rick's good friends that he had "spontaneously healed." Apparently, within hours of our healing session, he was feeling better, required no more pain medications and began eating again for the first time in a long while. He was soon released from hospice and returned home. I found it remarkable that neither Rick nor his wife called me to let me know how he was doing and that he had experienced such a profound healing. The session was never mentioned, even though I continued to do contracting work for them. Looking back, I think it was just too far outside his belief system to acknowledge that the Holy Spirit had performed a miracle in his life. With acknowledgment comes responsibility for faith.

Rick lived for several years before the cancer returned, though he never regained the use of his legs. He was able to spend time with his small children and put his affairs in order. But even when the cancer returned, he never asked for healing again. Through my friendship with June, I knew he hadn't dealt with his issues regarding his relationships and his faith. I believe this underscored a lack of desire to live. This is an example of how spiritual healing goes only as far as the free will of the subject and his soul allows. This is something spiritual healers must contend with when asked to help. We cannot be attached to the outcome, even if the patient is a close friend or family member.

Chapter Two: My Transformation

My experience with Rick had a profound and disturbing effect on me. Although I had a sense of the power of Spirit and what that power could achieve, there was still so much I did not understand. For one thing, I did not understand why the Holy Spirit would allow people to get hurt when using *its* energy to help others. Sister Sara, June and I were all hurt when we were thrown to the ground in the parking lot. The incident shook me up enough to make me vow never to use my "gift," or whatever it was, until I fully understood all its ramifications. However, life does not always go as planned, and there were times when I found myself having to use my gifts for my family. But whenever I did, there was always some kind of price to pay. I now know this was because I had more work to do regarding my spiritual growth.

Within two days of the healing session with Rick and Sister Sara, my four-year-old son suddenly became very ill. We rushed him to the hospital where an X-ray and examination showed an advanced case of pneumonia. In great pain, he was given two large shots of antibiotics and we were sent home with additional oral medication. The doctor told us to bring him back in a week for follow-up treatment, including more shots and X-rays. I called Sister Sara after we returned home and put our delirious, incoherent son in our bed. I told her how sick he was, and she offered to pray for him. She also encouraged me to lay hands on him, as I had done with Rick. Together we began a healing session on my son, my hands being guided to the proper places for his needs. I could feel and see the energy flowing around me to him, just as I had with Rick. When I felt the energy stop flowing, I let Sister Sara know, and we stopped the session. My son then fell into a deep sleep that lasted until the next morning, when he awoke feeling fine. His fever and pain were gone and all of his exuberant four-year-old energy returned. At our scheduled hospital appointment, the subsequent X-ray showed his lungs were completely clear, with none of the expected scarring. The doctors were amazed by how quickly and completely he had healed.

Sister Sara warned me that my son's illness was caused by the same energy that had thrown us down in the parking lot. She said "it" was "retaliating" for being removed from Rick and urged me to protect my family and myself by going to church every week and to have them all baptized. She believed the sacraments and community of the Church would provide the protection necessary for me to use my healing gifts. This didn't make sense to me, because I figured I was as likely to run into trouble within the Church as without. But I knew there was more to this process, specifically in the area of protecting myself during and after healing sessions. It became apparent to me the energy being removed from people had to go somewhere, and I saw that this energy had a vested interest in stopping me from performing acts of healing. I had an intrinsic knowing that I should protect myself from it, but I knew Sister Sara's suggestions weren't the answer. Again, my gifts were requiring me to search and to continue to grow spiritually.

It was less than a year later that our oldest son broke his collarbone playing flag football at school. He was taken by ambulance to the local emergency room where an X-ray confirmed the obvious and he was placed in a splint to support the healing of the fracture. The hospital made an appointment for us to bring him back in ten days. My son was in terrible pain and implored me to "make it better," so I decided to lay hands on him. This healing act had an immediate effect of healing the broken bone, reducing the swelling and alleviating his pain. Instead of weeks of immobilization and pain medication, my son was back playing flag football after three days. His teacher called and expressed the school's concern with his quick recovery and activity on the playground. I assured her he was fine and that his injuries were healed, although I'm not sure what they thought about how he came to recover so quickly.

Three days later, on the way to a local store to buy Halloween supplies for our children, our family sedan was rear-ended by a green Chevy pickup truck. As we sat there for a minute, getting our bearings, I realized my head and neck were hurting and my hands were becoming numb. My wife appeared to be unharmed. When the driver of the truck came over to tell us he hadn't seen us and that he was sorry for hitting us, I could smell the alcohol on his breath. Fortunately, the local police arrived and took over.

I was taken to the hospital, examined and X-rayed. The diagnosis was soft tissue damage between several vertebrae, which caused numbness in my hands and arms and the onset of terrible migraine headaches. Later, when I told Sister Sara about it, she expressed her belief that our car accident was related to the healing of my son's broken collarbone. I was questioning more and more how the use of my gifts impacted the presence of energy around me. I was learning that it was necessary for me to have some type of protection whenever I was being used as a healer. Sister Sara again informed me of her belief that the sacrament of baptism and joining the Catholic Church would provide the necessary protection. Since this still didn't make sense to me, our conversation propelled me to search for answers beyond the scope of knowledge available to Sister Sara. With each use of my gift, it became more apparent to me that I had to search for answers in order to use this gift at all, even for my own family. In this latest situation, Spirit had not removed harmful energy from my son; rather, it was the use of spiritual energy to heal his physical ailment that motivated interference, which was designed to dampen my desire to use my gifts. I later came to understand that these things occurred because it was important for me to learn that the use of any spiritual energy should be done only within the protection of the Absolute.

I began a search for knowledge and understanding that lasted for years. Sadly, it was mostly futile. Sister Sara gave me several books about healers, but they dealt only with "prayer healers," those who used the gift of prayer to request healing. What I needed was information on "command healing" in which a healer is used as a tool of Spirit, within the boundaries of free will, to change the physical, mental and spiritual aspects of life.

I visited several churches of various denominations and spoke with priests and spiritual leaders, without much luck. I saw that organized religion would benefit from opening its doors to the possibilities of these gifts and not see them strictly as ancient fables. I have heard many people say the Absolute does not hear our prayers in this modern world. This is not true. We have simply become a culture that turns a deaf ear to such possibilities.

I did have a few positive experiences during my search for truth. I had heard of a particular Catholic priest who was involved in the Charismatic Renewal movement, which started in 1967 when a handful of students and university theology professors from the Duquesne University in Pittsburgh got together for a retreat weekend. Now the movement includes more than 70 million Catholics worldwide. Charismatic Renewal focuses on the renewal of individual commitment to the person of Jesus Christ in His Church through the power of the Holy Spirit. Individuals within the movement believe they have been "filled" or "baptized" with the Holy Spirit, often through the laying on of hands. Signs of that baptism or filling may include any of the nine spiritual gifts described in the New Testament, 1Corinthians 12:8-10: wisdom, knowledge, faith, the gifts of healing, miracles, prophecy, discernment of spirits, speaking in tongues, or interpretation of tongues.

I went to a church in Seattle where Father Jose was giving a healing mass, and I saw that the Holy Spirit did, in fact, visit the service. I could see the energy swirling around the cathedral, not paying particular attention to any one person. This healing energy appeared to me then, and still does, as a beautiful, bright, healthy, sparkling green color. I was amazed as it swirled and sped about the cathedral. As this was the first time I had ever attended a healing mass, I did not know what to expect. During the service, I saw a person with some type of crippling disease and felt a great urgency compelling me toward him. It was similar to the anticipation we feel as we take off for our first airplane ride. So I sat behind this man, and I began to have an overwhelming desire to touch him, but of course I could not. I was far too shy about the direction I was receiving. As the service ended, I was still doing nothing with the energy flowing through me, seemingly searching for an outlet. This wouldn't have been so bad had it not been for the very painful stigmata marks that appeared on my hands and side. The redness subsided quickly, but the feeling remained there for about a week afterward. The marks manifested as a hot, red rash that peeled. I kept this to myself, but I was so upset about it that I left the service without directly meeting the priest I had gone to see! In the days to follow, I did not share this with anyone, not even my wife.

Father Jose soon went on an extended sabbatical, so quite some time passed before I was finally able to contact him. Eventually, when I did call him and told him my story, he was most interested and agreed to meet with me. At our initial meeting, we had a long discussion about what I thought was my gift. He agreed it was a gift but thought that I had many more. He asked me how I felt about the Catholic Church. I explained that I was not in entire agreement with the Church, as its laws were much too confining to God and man for anyone's spiritual gifts to manifest freely. At this point he explained the Charismatic Renewal movement within the Church and what it meant to the Church, possibly allowing the whole Church to grow and change. Its focus was on the individual's experience of God the Father rather than an individual's relationship with the Church itself.

I was amazed at the institutional growth that had taken place since I had last participated in any Church activities. I told Father Jose I was interested in this movement and its goals, and he asked me to take part in a healing mass he was holding in the near future. I was a little taken aback. I had come to believe that the Catholic Church didn't want anything to do with people like me, and I had long since written off the Church as buried in too much dogma. But this new movement intrigued me and, hungry to find like-minded people, I agreed to attend.

Then Father Jose asked me if I knew the root meaning of the word "holy." I said that it is someone who was picked to have extreme devotion to the divine. He explained that this was, in fact, wrong. He said the term "holy" means "separate."

"Eric, you will always be 'separate' because of the gifts you choose to use," he said. "You cannot understand why people just don't get it, why they keep searching for the answers that are right in front of them. You see this and experience what others cannot. Therefore, be kind and patient."

I appreciated hearing those wise words at that time in my life. They allowed me to relax a little about all the things that were happening to me.

When the time came for the healing mass, I had requested not to be identified or given any special recognition. If anybody asked, they were to be told that I was just a friend of the priest. Father Jose was happy to oblige.

Now, Father Jose is a very kind and caring man. He is a wonderful priest who serves his calling with passion and commitment, but even he would tell you that public speaking is not one of his best attributes. But on this day, when he commenced his sermon, I saw a huge angel appear behind him. The angel seemed to energize him, and he began to speak with great passion and clarity. The whole congregation was riveted, mesmerized by this unusually charismatic priest. The angel would periodically prod Father Jose and, each time it did so, Father Jose would get louder. He glanced at me with a look on his face that said, "What's happening to me?" It was fantastic to watch.

After the service, Father Jose asked me what had been going on while he was speaking. He freely acknowledged that he had never given a sermon like that before. He said that he had worked with a seer before and wondered if I had been able to see anything. I described to him, as best I could, what I had seen. The "angel" looked like an enormous gown with a head on top of it. It didn't have wings, as in the most popular depictions. It was huge, multi colored, and sparkling all over. It was laughing and smiling and seemed to be having such a great time that it made me smile and laugh as well. I had to contain myself because I didn't want to seem disrespectful during the service.

I told Father Jose that, when he would slow down or lose his train of thought, the angel would poke him, and that's when his oration would perk up again. He said he had been aware that something unusual was going on and told me it was almost unnerving, but when he found himself slowing down, he would get this surge of inspiration and energy, and wonderful words would come out of his mouth. I also told him I saw the healing energy of the Holy Spirit, which was bright green, swoop down through the church and move through him as he spoke. This energy would swoop down and go through a person in the congregation, then swirl back up through the high reaches of the church and swoop back down again through another person. I know these were people attending the mass to ask for individual healing. They had to have been open to the Holy Spirit in order for the energy to move through them.

I reminded Father Jose that he had asked for guidance from the Holy Spirit, and that was what I was seeing. He said he had been able to feel something working in him, almost as if he were being nudged by something, and then he would find himself literally filled with the words for his congregation. He definitely felt inspired as he spoke and was amazed at what I could see happening around him and in the church.

As the service progressed, the time came for various prayer groups to go to the front of the church to be recognized and take their places around the pulpit. The congregation could then line up in front of the prayer group of their choice and petition to have their prayers said. The congregation divided rather evenly among the four or five groups, one of which included Father Jose and me. I had never done this before and was already uncomfortable to begin with, but then it got really weird when individuals started collapsing in front of me. I would raise my hands to their chests and some of them would just drop to the ground! There are always people at these kinds of revival masses who feel compelled to be "slain in the Spirit," but you can spot them from a mile off. These people were definitely not faking it.

People from the other prayer lines saw what was happening and started to switch to our line. I began to feel a little embarrassed. They just kept coming. We were in line for almost four hours, but it was a delight to do such work, to see the people's faces. They were all wondering who this guy was with this newly energized priest. I do not know what took place within the people after the service, but during the service, people were at least healed by experiencing a tiny bit of the Holy Spirit's power. I saw each person's aura and the specific colors indicating issues, illnesses, and emotional well being. Knowledge came to me about what this all meant for each individual.

I saw the Holy Spirit swoop down and remove both physical and spiritual energy from which the person had already learned important life lessons. On a few occasions I received knowledge that the end of this life was near. I could also hear some of their desperate pleas for help which were not going to be answered because the forum for their healing was not this venue. I could hear the individuals cry for God to take away their pain. I later learned that removing a person's pain before they have learned from it bypasses their free will. The Holy Spirit will never remove or circumvent free will; otherwise the purpose of life is removed. But at the time, all I saw was the pain, which made me sad and gave me many more questions that could not be answered – yet.

A thought ran through my head many times during the mass: I hoped that any healing that did take place would be for the highest good. I also hoped this would not be "revival" healing, where people get some great results during the service, only to have the healing dissipate some weeks later because the root of the illness was not discovered and dealt with.

When the mass was over, Father Jose and I discussed what I had seen and what had happened to some of the congregation, and he told me about some of his prior experiences with Spirit. Unbeknownst to me, Father Jose had invited several priests to the mass to observe me. Apparently, some of these priests were also able to "see" as I do. He had hoped these priests would approve of my participation and acknowledge my gifts, as he wanted to have more healing masses with me and needed the church's sanction.

After he spoke with these priests, he told me they had given their blessing for him to work with me in further healing masses. I thought that was wonderful news because it felt like a validation of my gifts from a powerful outside source that, due to my upbringing, still had an influence on me. I happily agreed to participate in more healing masses and, over the years, have attended five. To this day, Father Jose and I continue our dialogue about spiritual gifts, energy and the Catholic viewpoint regarding these issues.

During my searching and questioning, I still had to pay the bills, of course, but my professional life was taking a nosedive. Soon after our car accident, I realized that my days of supporting my family as a contractor were over, because every time I tried to perform overhead work, I suffered a migraine headache. During my recuperation, my wife and I created a new business – real estate inspecting. This made good use of my skills and knowledge without the physical demands of my former work. However, a few years later a State Superior Court judge rendered a verdict that made inspectors liable for a structure for up to three years after an inspection. This put the insurance premiums up to astronomical levels for all independent contractors and ensured that anyone who stayed in the business would be spending more and more time in court and less and less time earning a living.

I really did not need that kind of stress, so I looked into another career change and began studying for the International Conference of Building Officials (ICBO) exam in order to become a residential inspector for code enforcement. Unfortunately, I am dyslexic, and, although I met all the other requirements, I kept missing the required exam score by one or two points. (I even corrected mistakes on their exam, but the bureaucracy of the examination's board failed to see how that contribution might offset a wrong answer here or there.) I guess I could have studied harder or pushed the exam board to make allowances for my reading disability, but my heart just wasn't in it anymore. I had been feeling more and more disillusioned with my contracting work as the years went by and, after the accident, it became even more of a struggle. The stress of my career upheavals was becoming intolerable.

But what could a guy like me do? The building trade was all I knew, other than how to heal people, and that's not a proper job, is it? I remember sitting at my kitchen table one dreary, cold winter morning, flipping through the Yellow Pages for inspiration. I got to the section marked "Career Counseling" and one ad in particular caught my eye. At the time, I couldn't tell you why I picked out this particular therapist's ad from all the others, but now I know that we were destined to work together.

I dialed the number a little nervously, wondering whether this person, Don, would be able to help me, and got an answering machine. I left a message and received a prompt response, including the explanation that the ad in Yellow Pages was an old one. This therapist had shifted the focus of his practice to psychotherapy, rather than career counseling. I explained my situation briefly, and he agreed to meet with me, explaining that underlying personal issues very often drive career concerns like mine.

I was relieved to find Don a pleasant man in a relaxed, informal setting, but I was filled with apprehension: I had never been any good at asking people for help. During our first session we discussed my career concerns at length. Don took notes on the historical information about my life, focusing on my education, work experience and skills. I told him about how I had become unable to continue working as a contractor and about how I had tried to become an ICBO inspector, but that my dyslexia and the governing board's intransigence prevented me from doing so. I suspected that this had all helped to create the funk I was experiencing.

Don listened carefully, taking notes, until, toward the end of our session, he asked me about my passions in life. It was then I mentioned a "small" detail that I had not yet entrusted to anyone. I could hardly believe it myself as I finally shared my most profound agony. Underneath my "normal" exterior, I was unhappy with all the "normal" things I had done. I had this huge desire to explore some of the nagging questions that constantly popped up in my life.

By this time, I was a 38-year-old family man with a small but successful business. I owned a house, a car and a truck, and had the outward signs of success as defined by our culture, but I was not happy. I had achieved these things through physical and emotional hardship. I had also survived a physically and emotionally abusive childhood, but I never gave up. Looking back, I had what I now realize were some very unusual experiences. In my youthful innocence, I didn't know they weren't part of everyone's experience. With maturity, I began to realize there were some pretty amazing things happening to me. However, this knowledge had eluded me in my youth in order to keep me safe. I had kept these things to myself, never really feeling any urge to bring them up. I know now that my entire youth was fraught with fear. There was no person with whom I felt safe enough to talk about these experiences. Sadly, I was denied a context for understanding these wondrous gifts. (This has come together in my life today – but not yet then -- as a strong desire to develop a safe place for all to explore their own gifts.)

Daring to trust Don, for reasons which became clear only later on, I told him that I had been used as a healer for many different people with what could be called astonishing results, and that I really wanted to explore that aspect of my life. But how could a mere man, obviously not well "put together" at this point, dare to call himself a healer? What was a healer? How does healing occur? How do I learn the "craft"? My mind was full of questions for which I had found no answers, but at last I had given voice to my deepest concerns. I had finally laid it all out on the table: the wondrous, amazing experiences and the hopelessness and loneliness they had caused.

Don became curious. He asked me why I thought I had been used as a healer. What did that mean? What does it mean to be a healer? What are the parameters of the gift? At last, here was a person with an authentic interest in why my life unfolded as it had and what might be intended for me. Don was an inexhaustible source of questions that brought together my gifts and my history, clarifying my life's purpose.

I explained that, although I had searched for them, I did not have all the answers, but I knew I was not a "New Age" healer. I was very clear about that. I had knowing and understanding that was absolute. I had learned to distinguish between pride and outright lies, and to recognize truth and integrity; I had even learned to recognize them within myself. I had learned that if I was not "in truth," I felt different, and I had to be constantly vigilant.

I was comfortable talking to Don and began to feel he might understand my situation better than I did. Over the course of our weekly sessions, I began to tell him about the various incidents throughout my life that had led me to believe I had a gift. Together, we began to recognize a pattern in my life of compassion and alleviating other people's pain. Don helped me identify the truth of the value of my life. He helped me to see the individual who had come through all the abuse from my brothers, my father and the unfamiliar, and realize that, in order to be happy within myself, I had to become comfortable with the individual who had been forged out of all the circumstances of that life. In order to be "me," instead of my father's and my brothers' ideas of what a man should be, I had to become what God's idea of a man is. I had to learn to ask for help from other people as well as from God. (Being naturally stubborn, this is a difficult one for me!)

Don earnestly encouraged me to pursue my life's purpose. He was concerned that I would not be happy in any career until I had explored healing in more depth. I was still not sure whether this was a viable career choice for me and was also concerned about the biblical paradox of charging for healings. Both Father Jose and Don were clear that I would be charging for my time, not for the service of the Holy Spirit. I knew nothing about how to be a healer, what the process was, or how to "set up shop," so to speak. Nevertheless, this "felt" right, unlike any of the other options in front of me, and, encouraged by Don, I took a leap of faith.

Making this change in my life was enormous for me. I had a

wife, three children and a mortgage. I had been a physical worker all my adult life, and now I was leaving behind all that I knew. I was venturing into an unknown field without any formal experience upon which to draw. There were no references or resources that I could find within our culture for what I was being called to do. I was creating my practice even as it was happening. But as soon as I started functioning in the capacity of a spiritual healer, my personal growth unfolded much more rapidly. As I allowed myself to accept my calling on a formal basis, I received new information daily. The gate to Spirit was opened more fully than I could ever have imagined.

Now I converted my contracting office into a healing room, making sure the space was peaceful and comfortable, and began to tell people about my change to a full-time spiritual healing practice. I was amazed at the very positive response I received from those who had previously known me only as a contractor. Interestingly, hardly anyone seemed surprised. It was as if they had been waiting for me to "get it." Quite rapidly, and mostly through word of mouth, people began calling me to set up appointments for healing sessions. I introduced myself in those initial phone calls and explained a little bit about what I did, drawing on my past healing experiences. I did not encourage clients to give me information about themselves or their circumstances, but told them instead that the way I worked was by being guided by Spirit. That was the best way I could explain it at the time. It's probably the best way I can explain it today. I also cautioned them that they could expect to get what they *needed* at that point in time, but that it might not be exactly what they wanted.

As I began to schedule appointments, I remember being as

nervous as a turkey at Thanksgiving. I thought, "What the hell am I going to say to this person?" People would ask how long the appointment would take and I would guess "an hour to an hour-and-a-half." I really didn't know how long it would take. I didn't know what to say or what to do, and I had absolutely no idea what the sessions would "look like." What was I supposed to do? I was petrified, but I decided that, as long as I was open to the guidance of Spirit and set my personal ego aside, everything would be fine (hopefully). In other words, I punted. Don reminded me that I would know what to say when the time came if I stayed connected to Spirit. He was right. The words were there as needed, and gradually I became more at ease.

Within a month, people began calling me with all manner of issues and concerns, everything from cancer to advanced arthritis, heart disease, blindness, and even infertility. As word of my practice spread, a local alternative health publication contacted me and asked if they could interview me for a feature article. I was surprised and happy to oblige. A reporter came to my office and conducted an interview, asking me about my gifts and how spiritual healing works. He even took my picture to include with the article. The article come out in the following month's issue and, after that, things really began to take off. Fortunately, by this time my practice was developing a kind of natural rhythm.

I was so busy that the practice became real, not some pie-in-the-sky dream, and I began to worry about whether there were any legal rules or requirements for practicing spiritual healing that I should be following. As it happens, in the state where I live, you need a minister's license to practice healing, and Don introduced me to someone who could help me get one. He also helped me with many other aspects of the nuts and bolts of my practice, including preparing a consent form for my clients in order to meet legal requirements and protect my family. I also began receiving referrals from naturopathic physicians, body workers, acupuncturists, psychotherapists and chiropractors.

During the healing sessions, clients lay on a massage table, and I made sure they were comfortable, perhaps giving them a blanket or pillow. Once they were settled, I asked the Holy Spirit for protection for both the client and me. I had never been to a spiritual healer myself and had never read a book about spiritual healing, but I had a knowing that I should ask for protection, especially after some of my earlier experiences with the "costs" of doing this type of work. So I proceeded in innocence and ignorance, just doing the best I could.

I then asked Jesus Christ (because this is part of my frame of reference) to lead the session and show me what the client needed. Christ Energy, or Logos, is the energy from the Absolute that Jesus demonstrated throughout his life. It is the compassion and love that Jesus experienced in his physical life that provided the road map of direct access to the energy of the Absolute. In my sessions, I used this energy to protect my clients and myself. It seemed to work very well, even though I was new to it all. I later learned that, as I was finding my feet, I was sent only clients who did not have a significant degree of energetic pollution; as my gifts awakened, the clients became more challenging.

I explained to the clients that, during the session, I would hold my hand about nine inches above their bodies, with my eyes closed, and would allow Spirit to move my hands in whatever direction was necessary. As an example, in one of my very early healing sessions, I found my hands over a client's knee. William had come to see me for a physical problem, specifically a depressed immune system. He was getting colds all the time, suffered from various allergies, and had a pain in his left leg that kept him from rowing, which he liked to do for exercise.

When I'm "shown" something, I might get an actual visual image, like looking at a photograph or a movie, or I might hear specific words or sounds, or it might be a combination of both auditory and visual information. I might also just "know" something about the place on the body where my hand is hovering. This would be information I would have no way of knowing otherwise. In William's case, what I was sensing included a knowing that the energy and pain in his knee were akin to those following an amputation. Since he quite plainly still had his entire leg, this seemed odd, but I told him anyway. William confirmed that he had a hamstring removed from his hip that was then used as a tendon for his knee. He was experiencing classic phantom pain in his hip, such as that experienced by amputees, in the area from where the hamstring had been removed, hence the energy I had sensed.

At that point I was shown in my mind a picture of a hamstring overlaying the gap in William's hip where it had been removed. I was "told" by William's Guides, or angels, that we could install an "etheric muscle" to replace the one that had been removed. (I will explain Guides and angels in some detail later. For now, think of them as my interpreters to the world of Spirit.) An etheric muscle is the energetic presence, or energy, of a muscle, which conducts the electrical signals to the brain. If the physical muscle is missing, an etheric muscle can be inserted energetically, so the physical brain registers nerve impulses as if the muscle had never been removed. I was truly surprised, because I didn't know we could do anything like that or what the results would be. Nevertheless, William's Guides installed an etheric muscle and his pain subsided immediately; he went back to his rowing.

William's healing continued with a degree of success until I noticed a pattern emerging. Whenever he became agitated with a female somewhere in his life, his allergy symptoms returned or he felt a pain in his right arm or leg, and his voice became weak. Every time the symptoms reappeared, he made an appointment with me and the symptoms went away again for a while; then they would return. I sent him to a chiropractor, who helped a little, but still, whenever confrontations of some sort came up, he continued to manifest the same symptoms. These interpersonal confrontations were not anything major; they could be as simple as someone in his life saying to him, "No, I think you need to do it this way," or possibly arguing over directionss to the gas station, just everyday male-female interactions. I saw this pattern emerge more and more clearly over a period of a year.

In order to prevent any misunderstandings or errors on my part as to information I was receiving from my Guides, I had purchased a few reference books on symbolism and had agreed that these would be our "decoder" books, for want of a better phrase. I was seeing William about every month or six weeks, and I suddenly began to see a clown at each of our sessions. I looked up clowns in one of the reference books and it said repeated clowns mean you need to see a psychotherapist. I recommended Don.

Don had not consulted with me prior to seeing William for the first time, so he took a history and talked about some issues, and William told Don about his work with me. One of the things he told the therapist was that I pointed out to him that every time he had an exacerbation of his symptoms it was because he had some sort of a run-in with a female. With that information, Don started to work, revealing that William had some significant early childhood wounds regarding his relationship with his mother, so Don began some EMDR (eye movement desensitization and reprocessing) treatment around those traumas. During that process, William was able to understand and release the pain of those early incidents. The trauma left him. The old, painful memories surrounding his mother's domination, the way she prevented him from speaking his truth, her refusal to honor the reality of his whole person, who he was as a little boy and who he became as a man – he was able to let go of it all.

William returned to me and, although Don and I had not discussed his case, I saw that his symptoms all related to an inappropriate energetic attachment, or cord, to his mother, which could now be removed because he had full knowledge of the energy's source and purpose. The energetic world is completely subject to free will. Only when we have full knowledge of any issue can it be worked on successfully. If we do not fully understand the issue, it will manifest again, as was happening with William. With full knowledge, we can freely make a choice whether we want to stay attached to something or not, but our choices have to be fully informed and understood before the energy of the issue can be removed permanently.

Now armed with knowledge and a willingness to let go of this attachment to his mother, William was able to let me take the energy of the cord, which I could feel in my hand, and mentally break it. I did this by picturing the Sword of Righteousness. It was a bit of an Old Testament type image, but it worked. The Holy Spirit was then able to repair William's physical and energetic body at one end of the cord, and the other end went back to where it came from. The effects were instantaneous and permanent, but not the end of William's treatment. Once that was cleared up, the Guides showed me the next level. While working on him and releasing the energy of whatever Don uncovered in psychotherapy, providing the initial release of symptoms, William's allergic reactions subsided for longer and longer periods of time.

Everything that happens to us emotionally and psychologically, as in William's case, gets stored in our physical bodies, because these incidents, like everything else in the universe, carry energy. Over time I have come to see patterns for our bodies' storage of specific types of energy. This is a similar pattern within all of us. The physical body holds on to the energy of some experiences because we need to explore and learn from them. This can keep us from repeating the same nonfunctional behaviors over and over. This is the part our bodies play in the education of our souls. This gift of the physical body is one, however, too easily dismissed in our culture.

During one of William's subsequent sessions, I saw an older man yelling at William. I described the man and William said, "That's my dad." I then looked into William's right wrist and was shown a woman. I described her to William and he said it was his mother. Her back was turned to him, even though William was looking to her to protect him from a giant beast which was his father. The images I saw also led to his left hip, where he had stiffness, because that's where we store relationships with males. I asked William to sign a release allowing me to share this information with Don. They were able to immediately begin processing the abuse from father and the abandonment issues from mother, which were both important aspects of his underlying distrust of females.

William continued in psychotherapy with Don and was able to identify an early childhood trauma related to that specific situation in which his father was abusing him and his mother was actually present in the room but looking away from him. Don and William processed that trauma and, again, once he worked through it, he was able to relegate it to memory, albeit a sad memory. Still, the energy of it had been desensitized.

When he came back to me, I was effectively able to release the energy I saw in his wrist and hip. It had been released before, but it had repeatedly returned because he had never dealt with the underlying issues causing the pain, which were emotional and psychological. Once he had that understanding, what the Guides had to offer him in terms of spiritual healing was effective and permanent. He had full knowledge and could then move on, free at that point to learn to have proper, balanced relationships with females as well as males.

This is a good example of what it means to do your "spiritual homework." William went to Don's therapy sessions to do his homework. It is also a good example of why spiritual healing works best if the healer is a medium or clairvoyant, clairaudient and clairsentient, as the healing can then be done with the client's full knowledge and participation. Successful healing also requires a heartfelt desire to release the inappropriate energy that we have learned from. William was able to get growth in every area. He apparently undertook psychological growth, emotional growth and spiritual growth and, as a consequence, he felt physically better. This is why his ailments don't return.

I now know that meeting Don was not only a blessing but also an essential part of my growth as a spiritual healer. We share common beliefs, a willingness to embrace the unknown, a total commitment to personal growth, and a deep spiritual belief.

Now, a couple years later, as I was contemplating writing this book, once again, it was my Guidance that kept prodding me to do it. Still, I hesitated, unsure and afraid of what the reaction to my book might be. My body would never let me get away with stalling. I began to suffer with excruciating kidney stones. I called Don and told him about the pain I was in and that I was racking my brain, trying to figure out why this was happening to me. I knew there had to be an underlying message, a purpose for the pain. Don said that to understand an event or behavior, it often helps to look at the end result. In my case the end result was that the kidney stones were preventing me from seeing clients. Bingo! It clicked into place. The message my body was giving me was that I should stop seeing clients, get off my butt and write this book.

After a year of creating a manuscript that was boring and far too intense for reading, I began to ask for outside help. I sheepishly asked Don for help. We discussed what I "knew" and questioned my Guidance, sometimes not finishing until midnight, until I had pieced together enough to send to my writing team, the body of this book. Along the way, my gifts opened up and developed because of the education I was receiving from my Guidance when writing this book, as well as the lengthy discussions about the research around this subject that Don and I were doing.

Chapter Three: The Blind Leading the Blind

I had been running my healing practice for less than a year, but things were already going pretty well, I thought. I had built up a reasonable number of clients and I was beginning to see some amazing things happening, including what could only be described as miraculous cures. However, I had no real frame of reference for what was going on, and so I was, to be honest, flying by the seat of my pants. When clients came in for a healing session, I would place my hands over them and my hands would somehow move to wherever they needed to go. I didn't know what was guiding them or how. I could feel what I thought were energies from each organ, and I could feel what I later learned were the energies of the chakras, but at the time, I didn't even know what a chakra was. I thought chakras were some sort of mythical Sanskrit theory. I had been taught not to believe in such things. I had seen auras, but, again, I didn't know what I was seeing. I didn't even know what questions to ask, even if I'd had someone to ask, because my dyslexia made it difficult for me to read about the things I experienced. Fortunately, help was at hand in the guise of a wonderful man who came to be one of my dearest friends and greatest instructors.

A reporter who had written one of the various articles published about me at the time called one day and said he had a friend called Bob who was a healer and a medium. Bob was dying and had requested to see me. Of course I agreed to the request, not only to offer whatever help I could, but because I was intrigued to meet someone else who called himself a healer. Not only was Bob a healer, but also he had the gift of sight, and I was bursting with curiosity, as I had "seen" things but did not know whether what I was seeing was a figment of my imagination or my own gift of sight. I did not yet think of myself as a seer/medium.

I didn't understand the full extent of Bob's condition until he arrived at my office, accompanied by a friend. He was totally blind, seeing only light as if through wax paper, and he could hardly walk at all, having to stop after every step to catch his breath. He also had suffered complete heart failure. He had undergone many open-heart surgeries, and his battered organ was of abnormal size and reduced to mush. As if that weren't enough, his kidneys were also failing, and his other bodily functions were gradually shutting down. A virus had caused all this damage. For most of us, this virus would have no long-term effects. For a few people who have no resistance, it can be instantly fatal. And for some, like Bob, who have a moderate resistance, it destroys the organs of its victims and they suffer a long, slow death. At this point the hospital doctors told him he had only a week to live, so he had asked to be discharged, as he didn't want to die in the hospital.

I didn't know what, if anything, I could do. Nevertheless, with the help of his friend, I got him up onto the massage table and let my hands move over him and be led wherever they needed to go. Bob was extremely sensitive and, although physically blind, he could still feel and "see" things related to energy. During that first visit we worked on his heart, because that was obviously urgent. My hands were brought up to his chest area and he started telling me about all the things he was seeing. He had been in the medical field for 20 years, trained as a nurse, and so understood how the body worked, and he described to me how, as my hands were moving over him, "angels" were working on his body. It was incredible. He started feeling better almost immediately, and a visible glow appeared in his cheeks, which had been pasty white up until that moment. He said he saw a huge energy coming from me and around me, and he described numerous angels that came into the room. He described his own angels, and then he described what he said were mine. This was the first time I had heard a description of what I now call my "Guides." I had "seen" them but had no reference to identify them. In the west we call these entities angels. In eastern mysticism they are called Guides.

We all have one master Guide or guardian angel, whether or not we acknowledge it. It is the part of Spirit that is always with us, and it is the entity that usually appears first. Our Guides appear in a form we can relate to because they are energetic beings without specific form. They adopt a form that speaks to our frame of reference, yet they will always appear first in their usual form so they can be recognized. My master Guide always appears first dressed as a monk, in orange robes with a little brown rope belt. He seems wise and jovial.

Bob also described for me twelve other Guides that appeared in various colors and with specific attributes. I have an unusually large number of Guides because I'm used as a spiritual healer. Most people I've worked on have from one to three Guides, depending on their needs at the moment. The number of Guides at your side will vary from time to time as you move through your life's challenges. This is of primary significance for all of humanity because it means we are truly never alone. It doesn't matter whether you are an atheist or not. It's not a matter of belief and has nothing to do with semantics, race, creed or sexual preference.

The Master Guide is reflected in everyone's primary personality. You will find evidence of your master Guide in your life, if you know where and how to recognize it. Once you became aware of your master Guide through a reading, you might notice how many things in your life are indicators of that relationship -- everything from your dishes and collections to the colors you picked out to paint your home. I notice my Guide's presence as my easy readiness to laugh and joke. I also have an ongoing knowing about things, which has really been a constant dialogue with my master Guide.

This was also the first time I had worked with anybody who had a connection to this type of energy. In fact, it was the first time I had met anybody who had a connection to Spirit similar to mine. Over the time I knew Bob, working together enhanced both of our gifts. I have since learned that cooperation seems to be part of the divine plan. No one is given all the gifts at once, but, working in cooperation, we can benefit from all of them. We each have different gifts, and when we work together with a common Spirit, everything is amplified and grows as our soul is educated from all types of interactions.

I was able to see just a little bit of what Bob said was going on around us, and I was a little bit wary, but excited at the same time. We started laughing and talking as if we had known each other forever. Any barriers that are usually between two strangers came down immediately. We were laughing at what he said the Guides were saying because, it turns out, Guides can be very funny when they're with people who have a sense of humor. (One time, when Bob and I were working together, my mind was off in another world and I wasn't paying attention to my Guide. He proceeded to show Bob and me, when I refocused again, an image of a mule's ass. This was my Guide's way of reminding me how stubborn I can be.)

I always ask my Guides to temporarily alter the way they appear to me, to be sure they are who they say they are and not something duplicated by dark or predatory energy. The first time I asked for this, my master Guide appeared as a dancing orange hippo with a pink tutu and a brown rope belt. Some time later, I was working on a woman with a very good sense of humor. We were having a relaxed conversation about what was going on in her session when the Guides had to get busy and do some physical healing. Perhaps because the woman had such a great sense of humor, they decided to capitalize on it. Suddenly, an old, wooden box, about two feet wide by three feet long, appeared. The Guides opened it and took out what looked like an old-fashioned white doctor's coat, which they shook, revealing a ton of moths. Then each of them put on one of those old headbands with a round mirror on it, which they had to clean off with Windex, and a pair of fake duck's feet. Get it? Quacks. The wooden box contained what appeared to be the contents of a Civil War field surgery kit, from which the Guides pulled out a rusty amputation saw. One of them pulled a dirty rag out of his pocket, spat on it and then wiped down the saw. Pulling down their surgical mirrors, they said, "We're going in!" I described their antics to my client and we were both unable to contain ourselves at the hilarity of it all.

I started seeing a little bit more of the things Bob saw, but I didn't trust them completely yet. There was one moment, however, when I got an unmistakable message from the Guides.

"Tell Bob this is going to hurt," they said.

I was a little taken aback. This was the first time I had received a message that loud and clear. I had received what I call an intrinsic knowledge before or heard utterances, but nothing this crystal clear. Still, I was not too happy with the message, because as far as I knew, this process was not meant to be painful, so I said to them, "No." Looking back, I suppose it might have seemed a little arrogant to argue with my Guides, but, hey, what did I know? I now know it's not arrogant at all, because we're supposed to challenge our Guides as this is how we learn to discern and trust. I frequently debate with my Guides as I continue to learn and grow as a healer. The argumentation is always for my clarity and benefit. They expect it. They are meant to work with our individual personalities, and some of us will question more readily than others, but we should all do it. This is how we learn and mature in our ability to discern positive energy from negative energy. There is no hierarchical relationship between Spirit and us. It is more like the relationship of two equals and dear friends. Spirit is not something to be afraid of. Fortunately, my Guides are infinitely patient with me, and they simply repeated the message.

"Tell Bob this is going to hurt."

I turned to Bob and said, "Bob, I've been arguing with them, but they told me it's going to hurt."

He went, "Uh-oh," and he felt something begin to "move" inside him.

The next time we met he told me that he had a bowel obstruction and that the Guides had removed it. In fact, he was a little too graphic in his description.

"It came out like having a baby," he said.

Ouch!

"Yeah. It was really painful," he said. "I'm going to believe you now when your Guides say it's going to hurt."

A week later he came back and we worked a little more on his heart and a lot on his eyes. I let my hands be led wherever they needed to go and, just like the last time, I started seeing fragments of what was going on around us – the Guides, or angels, working on Bob – but it didn't really mean much to me at that stage, and the picture was unclear, like a TV with bad reception. Bob could see everything as if in high definition, however, and so we were laughing and carrying on as he described to me what was happening. Suddenly, as I was standing by his head, looking down at him lying on the massage table, an angel appeared, as plain as day, face to face with Bob, hovering about six inches above him and looking straight into Bob's eyes. It looked to me like the bust of Michelangelo's Statue of David, with a white marble face that looked up at me briefly, then looked back down into Bob's eyes. This was Bob's Master Guide signaling to us that it would be addressing Bob's needs exactly as required. The angel appeared close to Bob's eyes because he could still see, as if through a pinhole, at about three inches from his face. He was quite startled when his Guide appeared that close, but he knew that it could see exactly what was going on with his body. There were other Guides in the room at this time, both mine and Bob's, and they all projected their energetic vibrations to the healing being conducted by the Master Guide.

Bob was excited because he could see what was going on and could feel what they were doing to his body, and he had some understanding of the mechanics of it, thanks to his medical training. We were both overwhelmed by it all. In fact, I jumped backward when the angel first appeared because it scared me. This was the first time I had seen something of the spirit world that clearly.

The next day Bob called and said, "I'm driving my car." His sight had been restored and he was feeling 100 percent better, so much so that, on the evening following that second session, he had gone out for a walk on his own, just for the exercise! To me this was incredible, as I had seen with my own eyes that only the week before he was all but dead.

During the time Bob was sick, he had been unable to work as a nurse, so had begun doing readings on people using his gift of sight. After he was healed, he knew they wouldn't take him back in the medical field due to the seriousness of his condition; his heart was still shriveled. So he continued taking on private clients. Every so often, though, he would see things that scared him or that he couldn't do anything about. He didn't have the ability to move large amounts of energy that didn't belong to him. He could slowly bring energy through his own body and use that to heal people, but it was like bleeding away his own life force, and his body could take only so much because it was still weak. So he asked me if we could work together on some of his clients. He used Don's term for me, "energetic power tool," and suggested I could be used to surround the energy and release it.

One day, a man named Andy came to see us and, as usual, we each did a reading on the client before the meeting. A reading is similar to meditating on a subject and allowing admission to whatever needs to come through. It shows us the main portion of energy that we need to deal with initially. It also gives us enough semi-personal information to gain the client's trust, developing confidence that there exists something beyond us. In this particular case, the readings we got were a bit unusual. At Andy's first session, he told us he loved all animals, particularly cats. One of his most beloved cats had died recently, and he was distraught. He had come to us because ... wait for it ... he wanted us to bring the cat back to life! Well, as you can imagine, we were incredulous but sensitive to his sincerity. What did this guy think we were? What was going on in his head? Clearly he needed tender, loving help.

Bob was directed to get in touch with the dead cat's energy to see what he could learn. The cat came back with a confusing message for Bob. It had no appropriate frame of reference to draw upon, so it just kept saying, "It's cold and dark and I can't get out. It's cold and dark and I can't get out," over and over again, in a rhythmic, almost poetic way.

Apparently, the cat was a reasonable size, and, as Bob was repeating out loud to me what the cat was telling him, the client said, "Well, it's in my neighbor's freezer." We just looked at each other, hardly able to contain our laughter, but we had to control ourselves. The client was dead serious. He actually wanted us to resurrect his cat. We saw that he needed to let go of the cat emotionally and psychologically so the cat's energy could go on to wherever it needed to go next, and so Andy could mourn and move on with his life.

A person's emotional and psychological attachment can hang on to a spirit, preventing it from moving on. I have heard of numerous cases of terminal patients in hospitals dying only when the family all leave to go have a cup of coffee. By leaving the room, they let go just enough to let the spirit loose. It's one of those quirky phenomena for which the medical world seems to have no explanation.

Our client's problem had begun with the controlling influence of his sister's narcissism. There were serious pieces of emotional work that needed to be looked at. The abuse that his sister's suitors brought into the very close family relationship was unending. This went on for years, and, while the boyfriends were with them, they managed to control every aspect of these vulnerable people's lives, even resorting to violence. They even hurt our client's dogs, cats and other pets in order to terrorize the family. Over time, our client came to place all his hope in his animals. It seemed they had become his lifeline to sanity. So when this particular cat died, that lifeline was severed and the man fell apart.

Over the course of several visits, we helped him let go of the cat, and the pet moved on energetically. I encouraged him to have a little ceremony to say goodbye properly and release any emotional attachments he might still have.

The more Bob and I worked together, the more I became aware that I "saw" the same things he was seeing, but in my own context. Gradually, I started seeing into the clients' lives, just as Bob could, but differently. By the time of our animal-loving client, about six months into our collaboration, I was being shown things very differently than Bob. I now know this was because we have different frames of reference.

Bob and I worked with one another occasionally. He was able to clear some things up in my life that I hadn't yet dealt with. That's when I first understood how episodes in our current lives affect us energetically and that we can release the energy from those events. Trauma, physical as well as emotional, needs to be learned from and released. I was beginning to understand this. Bob, however, seemed to be locked into his absolute, logical progressions. He would see some energy in a client that was causing them problems and say, "See, we can move this energy." But then I would see the same client again two or three weeks later, having re-manifested some of that same energy yet again. My instinct was to ask why, but I was in the back seat. Bob was the boss when it came to seeing, and he is very good at that, make no mistake, so I just took an apprentice role and watched. I would often be sitting there, observing a client, thinking, "This is a re-manifestation," and Bob would dig in and say to the client, "You've got to acknowledge this in order to let it go." Well, you can pound someone over the head with advice, but that's not the way the emotional system works. I had experienced enough psychotherapy to know you have to delve deeper, and the client has to have full knowledge of why this is happening to him in order to prevent it from recurring. Thus I began to see differences between how Bob worked and how I was being led to work.

I later learned that one of the big obstacles to Bob's not being able to see beyond his A+B=C model was that he was limited in his ability to help himself. He was willing to take only limited responsibility for what was going on with himself emotionally, and, therefore, spiritually, psychically and energetically, he couldn't go further than this with any of his clients. His personality was really quite open when working with others, but the fact that he was unwilling to deal with his own issues, beyond acknowledging them, was holding him back. If ever something came up that reminded him of his childhood, he would dismiss it instead of confronting it and understanding it, and that's how he dealt with his clients' emotional issues as well.

Conversely, I was very willing to deal with any psychological or emotional problems holding me back. Bob and I would work on each other, and he would see incidents from my pasts that were related to present-day issues. For example, I had been having problems seeing out of my left eye. It wasn't sight threatening, but my right eye was becoming increasingly dominant. Bob looked into my left eye and face and saw that my father had hit me there in the past. He saw that relationship and how I had been constantly disregarded and belittled by my father. My father's needs always came before mine. My left eye and face held onto a trauma so I would be keenly aware of how to stay safe when my father was in yet another mood. We were able to release some of the surface trauma because I could recognize the situation, and I no longer lived in this state of fear. I could not receive full healing until I later recognized and learned how this had affected me in the remainder of my life. At this time Bob could not understand my temporary inability to move forward, and therefore felt I was not accepting the healing. I was, in fact, accepting the healing, but it was the healing that was not complete.

When I was twelve, Dad took us to the coast to go deep-sea fishing. We started out from home very early, without stopping for breakfast, even though he knew I needed something to start my day or I would become ill after a short period of time. When I started to feel nauseous I asked if we could stop to eat. He refused, as usual, telling me it was "all in my head" and that I was weak because I felt sick. I ended up throwing up and becoming seasick on the boat, ruining the trip. This was typically how things went with Dad. My needs and my reality were dismissed and written off as "weakness." Had I really been weak, I would have begun to believe his version of my reality. As it was, I knew myself pretty well and didn't believe him when he put me down and demeaned me in front of my family and others. It was a hard way to grow up, but now I can see it made me more independent and intellectually curious.

On another occasion I was helping my dad put in a backyard pond and waterfall. I suggested he make the pond out of cement and, once it had dried, use mortar to set in the rocks. That way, when the cement pond expanded and contracted with the change in temperature, the rocks would not break free from the cement. He wanted to set the rocks directly into the cement and so refused my suggestion, telling me I didn't know what I was talking about. Basically, "shut up and work!" I didn't quite realize it then, but my Guides were showing me the whole pond construction and how best to accomplish it. We proceeded with Dad's method, which proved faulty, just as I had tried to explain. He would never try to benefit from my knowledge or help. He seemed compelled to put me down, belittle my suggestions and ideas, and pretty much discount me altogether.

On the other hand, whenever I worked on Bob and was shown an emotional issue that needed healing, he would usually decline, saying he already knew about it and had dealt with it. This was confusing to me because I did not understand why the Holy Spirit would show me something if it were not for the purpose of healing. I began to realize it was Bob who was not willing to do his work. I think this is why he never became his own "energetic power tool." Healing emotional wounds is an essential requirement for all, including spiritual healers. These processes help keep ego in check and help us turn our learned reactions into positive tools to help others. In dealing with any of these personal issues that Bob needed to process, not just understand, he would literally cut me off and refuse to deal with what his Guides were showing me. If he could release the energy of an issue at the moment, he considered it done. He did not recognize patterns of self-abuse and the re-manifestations that kept occurring to stop his life's awakening.

Each person has a unique frame of reference. My Guides showed me symbols that were different from the symbols Bob's Guides were showing him. They had similar meanings, but they appeared in a manner to which I could relate. Bob was the "master seer," so to speak, so anything I said was secondary to him. His visions were clear and absolute to him, but he didn't accept and realize that God works through all people, and when you work together, you can come from different perspectives, and your Guides can use those different perspectives to tell the whole story. His unwillingness to expand his frame of reference helped me realize our time working together was coming to an end. I began to see that my clients were not getting the full benefits of the spiritual healings because I was not heard during the sessions.

Having said that, it's important to be absolutely clear that my time with Bob was invaluable and that I could not have become who I am today without his help and guidance. His presence and feedback provided a safe environment for me to learn to really trust my gifts. This is a very important aspect of the learning process for all healers, and this is why we are meant to work together. Having this reference point, I learned to believe what I was seeing and therefore trust Spirit more and become a more useful healing tool.

All the lessons I learned from Bob were important, but perhaps none more so than the fact that it is so important for us all to work together and respect our different frames of reference. Our different reference points can help each in our personal development and different gifts. When we work together, we challenge each other, as long as we're open to the endless possibilities of Spirit.

Another great lesson I received while working with Bob was the need to protect myself when healing others. If a client had issues with something that corresponded closely with my own issues, then I could take on the energy from that client. Bob taught me how to ask specific questions regarding my protection. Working with Don has further shown me the benefit of innocent questioning in order to keep ego out of the process, thereby increasing the protection.

One particular client I was working on had problems with her father, as did I, and her energy was very similar to energy I had recently been healed of but from which I was still a little raw. I needed to do a bit more homework on the subject. (Looking back, I see I needed a bit of LI or Lifespan Integration. This is another tool for the therapist toolbox. By using LI, the Guides identify the individual traumas directly in the order that they need to be addressed, encouraging more powerful dialog within a therapeutic session.) When my client's energy was released, it jumped directly into me. This sounds somewhat dramatic, but it damn near killed me. Bob saw it jump into me and throw me back a little. I said to him, "I've got ten minutes to live. Can you close her energy system and come back and help me?" My heart was pounding so fast it felt like it was going to burst through my chest, and I had an absolute intrinsic knowledge that I had only ten minutes before this energy, which had grabbed hold of my heart, would inflict fatal damage.

Bob told me to go outside and try to ground in nature while he closed the gap in the client's heart chakra. I did as I was told and managed to hold things off for a few minutes. Bob helped me see what the energy was, and then I was used by my Guides to remove it. Instantly, I was back to normal.

It was all rather dramatic, but I learned from the experience a great deal about predatory energy, energy from creation, energy from the divine – and how our bodies function with it. I learned how to balance and use those energies, and that it is okay to use the energy from creation and the energy from Spirit to help me. They complement each other. We all have the same access to these energy systems, no matter what we call them and whether or not we even acknowledge them.

All energy, including what has been termed evil, or dark energy, comes from the divine source, the Absolute, if you will. I prefer the term "opportunistic" or "predatory" energy rather than evil. We've been taught all manner of beliefs regarding evil. These belief systems grant evil power that it does not own. The power of evil is, in fact, human fear. If you consider that all energy and all things come from the Absolute, then it follows that this energy is subject to the Absolute and held to its original intention. Also, and this is the interesting part, because all energy was created by the Absolute, it has a natural desire to return to the Absolute. This even includes predatory energy, which is cut off from that source. Biblically, this is referred to as the great battle of the heavens – Lucifer versus God. In reality, there was no battle. This energy left God's service of its own free will, marking the beginning of predatory energy.

The separation from the Absolute eventually created a longing for reunion, much as a child longs for her mother when separated. For predatory energy, this separation manifests itself as a desire to be in and control a physical body, which is something an angel can never do. In reality, this is a desire to have a backward connection to the Absolute through a physical body's connection. This energy wants to prey on the body-soul union, a human life, which is why it is "predatory" and has become "opportunistic." It wants to be in our energy field because it has an innate desire to reattach to the source, a connection we humans all have. The only way it can get this is through a host. This energy does not realize why it has such an overwhelming desire to be in someone else's energy field, but if it manages to get in, it can do considerable harm to its host in order to gain control and remain inconspicuous.

When a client shares an experience similar to one of my unresolved issues, I run the risk of opening a door through empathy. I am not able to help any client until I address the issues that are causing me to be vulnerable to this energy. Again this is why it is imperative for all spiritual healers to do their psychotherapeutic work for the education of their soul. I chose to seek professional help in order to work on my personal issues and resolve them, which now allows me to work with clients in compassionate detachment rather than empathy. My need for spiritual homework is ongoing, as things bubble up for me now and then just as they do for everyone else. The marvelous aspect of this is that I am constantly being led to resolve issues that can cause energetic weakness. This is always the way Spirit works. Nobody ever loses. That predatory energy would never have been allowed to enter me if I had not had Bob there to point out the way to release it. The situation would have unfolded in a different way or not at all. Without a safety net, I would not have been allowed to act as the healer to help this client in this situation. I know this to be true because similar things have happened many times since with no problems. Spirit will help you with your homework only if you're in a position to manifest it and heal it.

I stopped working with Bob after an experience with a client of mine called Dawn, who had originally come to see me for spiritual healing. After a few sessions I encouraged her to come and see Bob and me together, because I thought she might benefit from Bob's considerable gifts as a seer.

Dawn had already undertaken some psychological counseling in order to work on her issues, which included serious self-esteem problems, so she was well prepared for the spiritual steps she would need to take with me. She had attended about four sessions with Bob and me and had released a lot of energy that needed to be let go, but prior to her next session, when Bob and I did our customary individual meditations beforehand, Bob was still getting what I thought were overly dramatic readings implying that Dawn still had all this energy that needed to be released. It turned out that the symbols Bob was receiving were touching upon aspects of his own life that he had not dealt with because they were similar to Dawn's. When he communicated the images he came across, it was in a very adamant way because he was fighting his own denial. Because he would not face these issues in his own life, Bob was not receiving any greater understanding as they related to Dawn, and so he would not process, or encourage Dawn to process, the psychological ramifications of those issues.

The images I got from the same reading were much gentler and less dramatic, and they implied to me that Dawn had lost touch with her feminine side somewhere along the way. Soon after this, Dawn said that she did not want to see Bob anymore, and instead saw me on my own. It was during these sessions that I learned she had been abused, a fact that had been kept from me until Dawn was no longer working with Bob. She also had given up a child at birth and had an apparent unresolved longing for that child. As a consequence of these events, she didn't trust men, but was trapped in a cycle of gravitating toward men who were inherently untrustworthy.

Bob could see the pain in Dawn's life that had been caused by men, but all he wanted to do was release that energy, like a quick fix. I felt we had an issue that Dawn was willing to deal with, so we should explore it and see what needed to be done to eradicate it forever. Bob could not allow this during Dawn's session as this meant that his issues also had to be further explored.

Other clients I worked on with Bob also kept coming back with re-manifestations of their symptoms, so gradually I pulled away from him professionally and started to see clients on my own again. When I did, I had greater confidence in what I was seeing, which I owe to him.

Bob went to live in a remote rural location and just about dropped off the face of the earth, or so it seemed. It had been about a year since I had last heard from him when I had a prophetic dream. In my dream, I felt as if something was pushing on me in my brain. I could see someone's issues being presented to me as if in a movie, except there was also a feeling of physical pressure and emotional fear. I was actually experiencing someone else's fear and physical symptoms. I kept seeing a picture of Bob in a boat, drifting away from me. The next day, I felt irritable, agitated and physically depleted. The dream had been my Guides telling me to get in touch with Bob. Because I did not do so, they manifested the symptoms of irritability as a gentle nudge.

As it happens, I did not need that nudge, as Bob called me that day to say he was in the hospital, dying – again. He said he had contracted some bacteria and his organs were shutting down, so the hospital had him on emergency dialysis. Of course, his heart was still abnormally small, so that wasn't helping the situation. He begged me to come over there, so, of course, I took the next flight.

When I got to the hospital I started working on him, and immediately his kidneys started functioning again; the doctors decided he no longer needed dialysis. I worked on him for about three hours straight, easing some pain and a few other issues, and he started feeling a little better.

I saw him the next morning and worked on him again, but he just wasn't doing very well. I meditated on him and received a vision of a lesson I had learned in science years ago. I was shown a fresh human heart cell that had been removed from the total heart, and it just sat there and did nothing. Then another heart cell from another human was brought in and, when the two cells got close enough together, but not touching, they both started beating. At first they each had their own rhythm, but then they started beating together. When the cells were moved further apart, they stopped beating. They just sat there and died. The image then directed me to project my etheric energy onto Bob's body to get it to recognize a new pattern, one of life, not death.

Bob told me he wanted to let go. In his visions he could see a house up on the hill and wanted to go there. I was shown the same vision, but in mine there were still workers building the house. I told Bob to look more closely at his vision, which he did, and I said, "Well, who are those people?"

"Oh, those are workmen," he said.

"Exactly," I replied. "The house isn't finished."

With that, Bob acknowledged that his work in this life was not complete and that he needed to live, and he gave me permission to overlay the pattern of my etheric body over his. My Guides walked me through the process and I began to feel his body coming into rhythm with mine. I remained there for a little while until I was instructed to pull back. When I did, all his bodily functions improved and stayed that way. In essence, my energy was used to give his body new instructions.

This was only the second day I was there, and the doctors considered his recovery miraculous. I was planning to be there for a week, but my Guides said, "That's all he needs. You can do this from your house." And so I went home and arranged to project my life pattern, or rhythm, at a set time every day.

In about a month, Bob was discharged from the hospital. He stayed in a nearby hotel just to be cautious. Soon he went home and recovered to the same status of health he had enjoyed after our very first healing sessions together. Not long after, he called me up, practically giggling, and said, "I've been fired from all medical treatments." He told me this was because all his chemical readings and tests had come back normal for several weeks. He was elated.

Then I didn't hear from him for quite awhile – until he did it again. He had been having family problems that were causing his heart to shut down. He called me up, and my Guidance told me to do the same overlay. We did, and he completely recovered. By this time,

Bob's significant other had figured things out and said to him, "You know, Bob, you can do this yourself." So we worked on a few more things and then he disappeared again.

I have no hard feelings toward Bob or about going our separate ways professionally. Apart from being one of my greatest learning aides, Bob also became a very good friend, and my kids adore him. I am grateful to him and glad to have met him. We learned much from each other. He is moving in his own way, and his path has value. He has the ability to teach people to see as well as the ability to read past lives. This is as valid and wonderful as anyone else's life, including mine.

Chapter Four: Branching Out

Even before I met Bob, I had sought out therapy to relieve the persistent pain I was still having in my back and neck from my car accident. One particular massage therapist, Sherrie, was somewhat sensitive to spiritual energy herself and, after having worked on me a few times, asked what I did for a living. I told her I was a healer and that I had enjoyed considerable success with people. She was so fascinated that I ended up staying for an hour after our session, talking with her about it. I explained that, at the time, I didn't really know what I was doing, but felt I was being used to help people rather than directly helping them myself. Somehow she managed to sense the innocence in which I was working, recognizing that I was not a fake or charlatan, and she decided that some of her clients might benefit from what I had to offer, specifically those whom she had been unable to take any further with their healing process.

I told her about "balancing energy" or what I now call clearing. I was able to locate anomalies in the clients' energetic fields. In my practice I do not ask clients anything about themselves before a session. In fact, I specifically request they not tell me anything so that any preconceived notions will not influence me. I let my hands move over their bodies approximately nine inches above their form until my hands stop of their own accord. Typically I am shown an injury or an issue which has been bothering them in this area of the body. Then I tell them what I am seeing and, most often, I get confirmation from the client. In those cases I am usually guided to leave my hands over the injured area and change the energetic vibrations of that spot until it matches the rest of the body's energy. That usually alleviates the problem.

Sherrie began to refer clients to me whose problems she had been unable to relieve. I performed a clearing on them and sent them back to her for further treatment. She then told me that she was able to make huge progress with those clients, where previously they had been stuck for months or even years. It seemed that, after I cleared the energy connected to the underlying problem, the therapy she was doing would stick.

As we referred clients back and forth between us, Sherrie began to see the potential benefits of our working together on a daily basis, opening up so much more healing for her clients. She invited me to meet her at one of her smaller offices to introduce me to her practice and discuss the possibility of a closer working relationship. Although I am more than willing to cooperate with anyone genuinely trying to help people, as Sherrie is, and I was already learning that working with other disciplines produced greater results for my clients than my working on them alone, it was clear that Sherrie wanted to keep her practice the same as it was and just absorb me into it. She wanted to add to what she already had, instead of learning what she didn't have and growing into her gifts, which were considerable. For example, although she was sensitive to energy, Sherrie was unwilling to look at how and why she took on predatory energy when working on her clients. She ran the risk of taking on predatory energy through her own energetic weaknesses, and she was unwilling to learn how to heal the weak points in her energy field and cleanse herself energetically between clients. Thus, she was literally passing on predatory energy from one client to the next.

When I made Sherrie aware of this, she was open to changing some aspects of her practice, and she got better at setting energetic boundaries within her therapy, but she refused to see what was going wrong energetically within her practice and how, by taking on that unhealthy energy, she was adversely affecting her patients. To do so would have required her to rethink the way she saw herself, her entire practice and her place on the planet. She was stuck in our society's constraints that dictate that if you've got a successful business, plenty of money and all the things money can buy, then you've arrived; you're a success. Once you think in those terms, that's the end of growth, both physical and energetic.

Sherrie has the potential to be a great healer, but she is absolutely, willfully and consciously stuck in what society has dictated to her and, in particular, unduly influenced by her parents. They wanted their daughter to get married and raise a family and live a traditional life of mother and wife. Strong-willed, she rebelled against her parents' wishes by developing her own practice. She was a very independent and successful businesswoman and had no interest in marriage or family. So her outward signs of success, her flourishing massage therapy business, showed her mother and father that she could succeed in spite of them. Consequently, she has a huge vested interest in hanging onto everything the way it is to maintain that validation. I understand and sympathize with her position, but I declined her offer to join her, as I want to work with people who are not limiting their own gifts through the dictates of their ego or restrictive cultural mores.

Sherrie and I still refer clients to each other, and I have three other therapists with whom I work closely. Two of them are also energetically sensitive, and one is not. But even the one who cannot see the release of energy I achieve with his clients is able to feel his patients moving forward with their therapy once I have worked on them, and so he continues to work with me even though he doesn't fully understand why.

The experience of working with other healing modalities really opened up my eyes to the possibilities that cooperation can produce. This was validated even further when I began to work with John, a psychotherapist who had heard about me through a chiropractor who had referred clients to me.

John had been working with one particular client, whom I will call Dale, on several self-esteem and personal identity issues. John came to me a little frustrated because he had been seeing Dale for two years and had made great progress in the first year, but was now stuck at a dead end. They had been dancing around the issues for the better part of twelve months but just could not get in. John sensed there was something blocking Dale that he couldn't reach. Not only was that tough for the client's personal growth, but it was also getting very expensive for Dale, so John asked if there was anything I could do to help.

As I began to work with Dale, it quickly became apparent that he had issues with how other people identified with him and how he presented himself to the world. Later, I would be able to identify these as second chakra issues.

As usual, I had asked John and Dale not to tell me anything about Dale's situation before our session, but when I mentioned what I was feeling, he said, "Exactly. That's what I need to work on." Now with his explicit consent, my Guides showed me that he was an only child, had been very protected, and had taken on his mother's issues with identity. A parent can teach a child only what he or she knows, and so his mother taught him her hang-ups. He was unable to identify with who he was as a man because his mother thought a healthy male was unclean, something to be afraid of, something dark. He internalized her beliefs and absorbed their negative energy. As a consequence, unhealthy, or culturally obtuse, patterns emerged in his behavior, because he believed the very essence of who he was to be unhealthy. It's similar to a 17-year-old who can't legally have a beer. He wants it all the more because it's forbidden fruit. If a man is forbidden to be who he is because it's "dirty" to be a man, then we arrive at what our culture calls perversions, that is perversions of personality and behavior.

If we disregard our culture's restraints for a moment and examine what we are, as humans, we can see that we each have certain basic biological imperatives: to eat, to find shelter and to procreate in order to continue the species. Men and women are equal in every way, but we have different roles to play for the survival of the species. When we let fear dictate cultural norms, we end up damaging our well-being, and this is what I saw in Dale.

In Dale's case, his male identity and some of his natural male urges were, in effect, driven underground by his mother and her interpretation of cultural norms. The effect was that he turned to pornography as an outlet for his repressed sexual urges and became addicted to it. He felt a great deal of shame about this behavior, which grew out of the shame he had internalized regarding his maleness, but felt powerless to stop it.

I looked into Dale's second chakra and saw that it was very out of balance, very mixed up. I saw his own energy, and I saw energy built around someone else, a woman, whom I described to him.

"That's my mother," he said.

"Well, she appears to be like this and like that," I responded, describing the traits I could see.

"Oh, yeah. That's exactly the way she is," Dale replied.

Then I was shown incidents in his life where his mother had bestowed her beliefs about men upon him. He was carrying these around as energetic beliefs, making them major blocks around which he had constructed his self-identity.

When I described some of these incidents to him in detail and discussed the consequences of them for him as an individual, he could see this was no longer what he wanted. He was a married man at this time and knew that he needed to change in order for his marriage to survive and flourish. He was able to acknowledge the energetic blocks and ask that they be removed. Once he had exercised his free will, which is essential for removing predatory energy, I was able to remove that energy.

But that just cleared the energetic block. It did not retrain the mind. At that point, Dale went back to John, and he could then understand why he hadn't been progressing with his psychotherapy. Once again, he could actually hear the words, his own as well as John's, and he started to move on and have breakthrough after breakthrough. It was almost as if, before clearing his energetic blocks, he had a blind spot, and all the therapy in the world couldn't seem to get him to put it together in a conscious way.

Catherine, a naturopathic physician who practices acupuncture, heard about me through another naturopathic physician. She recognizes how well energetic medicine works in symbiosis with other modalities. She had been having problems with Tom, a patient of hers, so she had him call me. Again, this was before I had learned with Bob to really see how healing worked, so, when he came to see me, I just worked wherever my hands were directed to go. Practitioners of acupuncture and naturopathic medicine recognize what are called the meridians of the body, or channels of physical energy that flow through it, and my hands were led to Tom's kidney meridians, which are responsible for the kidneys, the adrenals the thyroid etc. The message I received was that they were totally blocked. They had a strange energy around them. For about an hour I was instructed to keep my hands in that area until everything balanced with the rest of the body. During this time, Tom said he felt all kinds of energy within him moving around, and he even saw some light and felt things flushing out of him. He was obviously very receptive to this type of healing, so I taught him how to move energy out of his body, down through his feet and into the earth. Then I taught him how to bring energy down from Spirit through his crown chakra and into his body.

About a week later, Catherine called to tell me she had been seeing Tom every week for a year and had gotten nowhere, but after his session with me, all of a sudden he was feeling much better. She said his kidneys resumed correct functioning, as did his thyroid. He felt great, and he no longer needed any of the supplements he had been taking for years.

When Catherine was interviewed for a magazine article about me, she correctly stated that energetic medicine works very well in conjunction with other forms of healing, and I would never disagree. Any healer who says you should do only one thing is acting as God. It may be that you need only one particular type of healing, but that should be left to the individual, not the healer, to decide.

Acupuncture is similar to energetic or spiritual healing in many ways in that the acupuncturist apparently tries to balance the physical energy of the body by tweaking the nervous system at acupuncture points. It has been my experience that these points will react to a needle, and the acupuncturist has to determine which acupuncture points will be most effective in helping clients alleviate their physical symptoms. It appears that the needles somehow manipulate their physical energy so the body can heal. The acupuncturist has to first discover a series of emotional and physical symptoms from the client in order to make the proper analysis of the acupuncture points.

When we do energetic medicine, we are also shown the physical energy of the body. The healer will find the same parts of the physical energy system closed down that an acupuncturist might find, although the spiritual healer/medium does not need to take history because spiritual healing does not rely on an intake of data from the client. A healer would just be led to the appropriate points that need work, as I was with Tom.

Where the two methods differ is that, in acupuncture, the practitioner looks only at the specific point where the problem lies, whereas a spiritual healer looks at a different picture, showing how those similar points got to be blocked in the first place, the underlying causes. For example, if someone was injured in an automobile accident, he might receive the best physiotherapy and acupuncture and even chiropractic help, but might still not be able to turn his head a certain way until the energetic trauma of that injury is released, because the body is still stuck in a protective mode. Spiritual healing will release both the energy and the cellular memory of that trauma and allow the physical healing to take place more permanently and effectively and allow other modalities of healing to be more effective. Many people still consider naturopaths, acupuncturists and even chiropractors to be practicing "fringe" medicine, despite the overwhelming evidence of their efficacy. I have enjoyed great success working with all of them, but I have also had success working with the patients of traditional medical doctors.

In one particular instance, a patient came to me with an elevated blood count in a range apparently indicative of some sort of cancerous tumor. He had an obvious growth that could be palpated from the outside. This man actually worked in the lab of the local hospital, so he fully understood the ramifications of his condition and had been scheduled for surgery to remove the lump on a Monday morning. The soonest I could see him was the Friday before, so he came to me, somewhat pressured by a relative, to see if I could help with the trauma of the upcoming surgery.

As usual, I didn't know anything about his condition beforehand, but sure enough, I was guided to the lump and worked on it for some time. My Guides told me to have him come back the next day and work on him some more, which I did, and then they gave an unusual directive. They asked me to have him request more blood work immediately before the surgery. They did not suggest that he cancel the surgery, because Spirit would never suggest anything that takes away someone's free will or interrupts the individual's process. Nor would Spirit ask a healer to recommend a course of action that would put someone in jeopardy. But they said that he might be interested to see the results of the tests. He said, "Sure. I can do that." So he got his doctor to order the same tests, just before the surgery, which had originally indicated his condition. The numbers had dropped down to almost normal.

He decided to go ahead with the surgery anyway, and they removed the lump and discovered it was benign. He came to me the following day and we removed the trauma of the surgery caused to the body. Within three days he was completely healed. His doctors were amazed. He reported that: 1) There was no infection; 2) the scar from the surgery was almost nonexistent, having completely healed; and 3) he got all his energy back almost immediately. Right after our post-surgery session he said that he had no more side effects from the general anesthesia or pain. This was the day after surgery! He indicated that all his bodily functions had returned to normal and all pain from the surgery went away so completely that he declined pain medication.

This man called me a few times to give me reports on his progress. I guess, as a man of science, he was amazed at the results. I have to admit, I am always a little amazed, too, but I have learned that science always proves out true spiritual healing. Spiritual healing is not magic. It is, or should be a natural part of our lives and used in conjunction with all the other disciplines that we have learned to use to heal ourselves.

Although just about all healing modalities can be beneficial, unfortunately the same is not true of all healers. Hans came to me fairly early on in my practice. He had been a medical student who had, over the course of the previous year, been forced to quit his life's passion because he was … well, no one could actually figure out what was going on with him. He could no longer pay attention in classes, where before he had been an excellent student. He could no longer hold a conversation with anyone, where before he had been outgoing and intelligent. He developed shakes, and he had violent mood swings. His doctors first thought he might have a brain tumor or perhaps have developed Parkinson's or some other neurological disease. They ran every test they could think of but could never find any physical reason for his sudden difficulties. It was a terrible mystery, and all the more tragic because Hans was just a very nice man.

Before his appointment, I was instructed by my Guides to protect myself. They told me to invoke Spirit and ask for its protection before Hans came. Although this was not a common occurrence in my practice at that time, it was not unprecedented, so I did not think too much about it and did as I was instructed. It was a good thing that I did because, when Hans lay down on the table in my office, the room immediately got significantly colder, even though it was a warm spring day. The temperature must have dropped by at least 15 degrees, because the heater in my office kicked in. As I connected with the man's energy, the room just filled up with it.

Although my gift of sight wasn't fully developed yet, I could see what looked to me like a big, dark cloud. Hans groaned as this energy came out of him, and I asked Spirit to protect me and to surround this energy and discover whether we should get rid of it. All kinds of moans and groans were coming out of Hans, who later was unable to remember any of this, as he seemed to be in a kind of trance.

My Guides instructed me that we absolutely needed to get rid of this energy, so we did. Immediately the room started to warm back up again, but it took about ten minutes to get back to normal.

The Guides then showed me that Hans had gone to an energetic healer a year before, a Reiki practitioner. Reiki is a method of natural healing based on the application of "Universal Life Force Energy," which is what Reiki means, literally. Its origins are somewhat in dispute, some people claiming it can be traced back several thousand years to Tibet, and others believing it began with Dr. Mikao Usui in the mid-1800s in Japan. Whatever the truth, it is generally accepted that Dr. Usui was the father of current-day Reiki practice.

Reiki apparently involves the transfer of energy from practitioner to patient to enhance the body's natural ability to heal itself through the balancing of energy. When practiced correctly, Reiki can be an effective healing tool and, by the way, it feels great too. I had it performed on me because I wanted to see what it felt like, and it was like getting a massage without anyone touching my body.

But just as in any other discipline, there are good Reiki therapists and there are not so good Reiki therapists. The person Hans had gone to was obviously good in one respect: she was able to manipulate enough of his energy that it apparently had made him vulnerable. (I was not present at the session, but I was shown this.) Unfortunately, while the therapist had Hans' energy fields open, some predatory energy that had been hanging around in the therapist's office saw an opportunity and, Bam! In it went to poor old Hans. There was no evil intent on the part of the Reiki practitioner; she simply did not know, nor could she "see" what she was working with. In this case, Hans apparently had some sort of hole or deficit in his energy, probably caused by a trauma or an issue, and the predatory energy simply flowed into it like water flowing downhill. He literally took on a possession, just as described by the psychiatrist M. Scott Peck in his book *People of the Lie* (Touchstone, 1983) and the theologian Malachi Martin in *Hostage to the Devil: The Possession and Exorcism of Five Contemporary Americans* (Harper San Francisco, 1992).

Both Peck and Martin, two highly respected scholars, describe numerous instances of what they call demonic possessions and write in intricate and often dramatic detail about the process of exorcisms to free the afflicted persons of their demons. In my experience, however, freeing a person of demons, or predatory energy, is a much simpler and more relaxed process. In Hans' case the guides showed me the predatory energy and where it came from, so I knew it was opportunistic. I was then used to bring the energy of Spirit into the room to protect Hans' physical body as well as my own.   Bringing in Spirit's energy of protection was something Sister Sara had taught me in the early stages of my work as a healer. She could sense this energy as it swirled around while I worked with people. Energy from Spirit, which sometimes appears bright green to me, enters the process and, with the free will, full knowledge and permission of the client, the predatory energy is then told to leave. It is surrounded by the energy of Spirit and is lifted up and moved through a portal that has opened up to source, or the Absolute, where it is transmuted and cleansed.

Because all predatory energy desires to return to source, which is why it enters a physical body in the first place, it complies with this process. There is usually no arguing involved and, once surrounded by the light, the predatory energy goes quickly. However, if the healer and the client have not fully discovered why the energy is present in the host, the energy won't leave. In other words, I need to ask to be shown all the information relating to the energy so the clients can have full understanding of their situation and how they came to take on this energy in the first place.

This is informed healing. This is an exorcism performed the correct way. This is the gifted spiritual healer/medium at his or her best. There is no prayer, badgering or "fight with the devil." And the client does not suffer or spew green vomit. Performed in any other way, it is much less effective, and the client will suffer, as will those performing the exorcism. This is one of the major differences between healing by command performed by a seer and healing by petition or prayer. So, having identified that Hans had no emotional attachment to the energy, I was able to simply clear it from him. If it had come from a childhood trauma, for instance, Hans would have had to work on the issues surrounding that trauma before recovering fully. In this case, the Guides told me that within six weeks he would again have his ability to speak and his life would be back to normal. Why six weeks when Spirit can fix anything in an instant? Actually, I don't know the answer to that question, but my Guides frequently put some kind of time- frame on a person's healing. My belief is that it takes a little while for the physical body to catch up with the spirit, or soul. In Hans' case, he was able to resume studying immediately after our session and could walk perfectly fine again within a week, but it was six weeks to the day before he regained full control of the motor functions of his mouth and was no longer prone to outbursts or social ineptitude. Perhaps the Guides knew that Hans would not be returning for the follow-up sessions needed for direct healing of the effects of the possessions, thus possibly requiring six weeks for the body to heal itself. It also might have been that six weeks fit within Hans' belief system.

Hans' story is a perfect illustration of a practitioner doing something with good intentions but without enough knowledge. This can happen through poor training, lack of knowledge, laziness, apathy or ego. I know from speaking with other Reiki practitioners that during the course of their training they were taught how to protect themselves and their clients from what I call predatory energy. Perhaps this particular therapist didn't pay attention fully. Perhaps she didn't believe in everything she was told. Perhaps she didn't think she needed to do things the way she was taught. Perhaps her main concern was to make a living. There's nothing wrong with making a living from healing; after all, medical doctors do very well at it. But if you are going to affect people's health, you had better know what you are doing in your chosen discipline. That applies to medical as well as "alternative" practitioners.

In the spiritual healing profession, people who fail to do their homework give the rest of us a bad name. There are no formal rules or ethics in spiritual healing, and no governing body like the American Medical Association. This results in a lack of accountability, without which there is no feedback for practitioners or healing systems from which to grow and learn. Effectively, this means that the circle of learning is closed, limiting the effectiveness of various energetic healing modalities. Without accountability, healers are unable to learn from their mistakes, which would help them grow in their skills as healers. A byproduct of this is the lack of trust in the spiritual healing profession as a whole from the general public, one of the reasons that healing is not more widely respected and used.

It is important to examine the relationship between spiritual healing and religious doctrine. In my search, I have found within each major religion a beautiful spiritual heart known as its mystical tradition. Spiritual healing is a fundamental experience inherent within each of these traditions. It makes me wonder why spiritual healing has become an outcast child of current religions. The Absolute is the foundation and heart of spiritual healing. It is the reason we have spiritual healing. Once again, I believe it's our investment in our version of the Absolute as the "true" version (religious doctrine) that has distracted us from the heart of the common experience of the Absolute. Spiritual healing is non-denominational. All the major religions declare their God as truly omnipotent, and therefore one would expect spiritual healing to be well within the realm of opportunity. To me it seems as if the various evolving doctrines are not able to allow for the promise of spiritual healing found within their own religious heritage.

You can sit in a church full of people, as I have, and, when the minister asks how many people have had direct experience of the Holy Spirit, almost no one raises their hand. How can this be, considering we cannot live more than a moment without experiencing Spirit in our life in one way or another! I wonder how these people can profess to believe in burning bushes and the parting of the sea but not in current-day spiritual healing. How can they believe that God interacted with man only 2,000 years ago and prior to that? What happened after that? Did God die? Did God stop communicating with us? Or did our social concepts become so rigid that we are no longer willing and able to hear God?

Spiritual healing is about a direct relationship with God and a direct relationship with the Holy Spirit and, as such, it is not confined

by any religious doctrine or science. That should make it a good thing -
- equal access and all that -- but, because most of the planet has been
brought up to believe in some particular view of God created by one of
the major religions, most tend to regard anything outside of that view
with suspicion.

I wonder why we seem to be constantly separated from a direct
relationship with the Absolute. One of the ways this is done is by
devaluing the individual's life and the importance of its cycle. Our
politics, religion and economics seem to foster this separation, which in
turn hinders our soul's progression. The soul can progress only within
the limits of the particular belief system of the individual, which, by
definition, has constraints. I must again underscore the importance of
direct experience of the Absolute. This is the foundation of spiritual
healing. It has been my direct experiences of the Absolute that have led
me on my journey as a spiritual healer and which have fostered my
personal psychological growth. Spiritual progression and my gifts of
sight and healing unfold together. I believe this is the way it is meant to
be. Otherwise, if one's emotional and spiritual progression does not
coincide with the opening of one's gifts, one is vulnerable to ego and
opportunistic energy.

I understand how spiritual healing is a threat to politics and
economics; it does not conform to the laws these disciplines represent.
It gives people a direct relationship to the Absolute and, therefore,
control over their own well-being. When you develop spiritually, you
realize that the things you used to consider important such as religion,
politics, economics and cultural norms, are secondary.

We have not yet developed the appropriate language to discuss
spiritual healing, and one of the consequences is that the human race

has been slow to grow spiritually. If we were more developed spiritually as a species, healing would be commonplace. All of the societal and cultural constraints against healing would be out in the open and discussed from a very early age, just as we teach little children today about religion. It would be a natural, innate process, and part of everyday life.

If little Johnny broke his leg, we would take him to a doctor to have it set, then take him to a healer to remove the physical and spiritual trauma so the injury could heal faster. If someone received an injury to the head that manifested in psychoses of some sort ten years down the line, the psychologist would say, "Well, have you ever had any head injuries?" and the patient would reply, "Well, yeah. When I was a kid I fell off my trike and hit a rock." The psychologist could then recommend having a healer remove the physical and energetic trauma of the injury so the body could heal organically, and then set about healing the psychological aspects of the trauma, all as part of the same process.

It is not by accident or chance that healing works with every other modality. God or Spirit or whatever you want to call the divine did not give us a brain not to use it, to sit back in an easy chair and say, "I'm sick. Heal me." We have a brain in order to find antibiotics, to find acupuncture and other healing modalities, and to use them in conjunction with energy.

On the one hand, it is somewhat refreshing that more and more people are seeing the shortcomings of traditional medicine and traditional religions and are searching for something that contains a more complete truth. Unfortunately, even the New Age movement, where many of these seekers end up, can be limited by ego and secondary gain. When people identify their worth through their gifts, they're not willing to look at how they need to grow those gifts. The New Age has no framework from which to work. It has no context. So the next guru or the next seer who comes along can say, "Hey, you have to do it this way, because look what I can do. Look what I can see." The guru may be gifted in some respects but limited by over-investment in his or her own abilities. (This fact includes me, so I constantly depend on others to teach me and keep me in balance.) And the seekers accept this small, limited demonstration of Spirit as absolute because most people are looking for an easy answer, a quick fix for their physical needs. That is why I believe it is important to look for spiritual healers who function within some type of tradition, some type of ancient belief system or frame of reference other than their own. In other words, be skeptical of spiritual healing according to Slick Rick.

A friend and I met a "channeler" not very long ago who fits this pattern perfectly. This channeler would connect with an entity, which we will call Ralph, on behalf of clients who would pay great sums of money in order to hear from dead relatives or learn about the future or whatever. Ralph was very good at this, and this channeler became quite famous on the West Coast for her ability to summon Ralph at will, and she was proud of her talents.

The channeler has never questioned the motives or intentions of this entity because it strokes her ego in order for her to allow it to come into her body and push her soul away. Ralph courted her and it convinced her that she would benefit professionally and socially. Her ego was weak. Ralph found a way to validate her as a person, and being a skilled channeler suited her. We asked her whether she knew where Ralph came from, or what energy it was that she was channeling, whether it was from the Holy Spirit or opportunistic. The great thing about energy is that it has to show its true colors if challenged. It cannot lie. She said it must be from the Holy Spirit because it felt good, because it helped all these people. But she never challenged it. She never even thought to ask. Maybe we planted a seed; maybe she will ask it at some point, but I suspect she is afraid to ask for fear of losing her meal ticket and claim to fame. She never understood that the spirit of Ralph was coming in and taking away her free will. When we asked her where her soul went when Ralph was in her body and she was speaking in Ralph's voice, she said she didn't know.

But again, her negligence wasn't out of malice. It was out of ignorance and ego. Ralph totally took over her body and interrupted her will to exist. This causes a break in the sacred body-soul union, and nothing from the Holy Spirit would ever do that. When Ralph takes over her body and forces her soul out, she loses free will altogether, and at that point her physical body is literally a channel, and that entity, that energy, can say and do whatever it pleases. It could kill her if it wanted to.

Another clue that Ralph was opportunistic or predatory energy was that he required her to perform all sorts of rituals before he would enter her body. She had to fast for a certain amount of time; she had to do a ritual cleansing with a particular kind of salt bath; she had to tie her hair up a certain way and wear only a particular white robe. The Holy Spirit does not need a body through which to communicate and would certainly never deny the functions of the body it helped to create. Spirit can work anywhere at any time on the planet. It doesn't follow that it would demand specific ritualistic behavior or a ludicrous routine from anyone. God does not interrupt free will. That's the one cardinal rule God has given him-, her- or itself. Free will is manifested in the connection between the physical and the spiritual, the body-soul union, and when that union is compromised, you know it is not of God.

Everyone is sensitive to energy, both predatory energy and light energy, or energy from Spirit, but because we have no language to discuss these things, and because society, through religion, politics and economics, trains us to be wary of anything outside of society's norms, we have never learned how to discern between good, spiritual energy and predatory energy which can feign good feelings. Consequently, anyone searching for identity or meaning can easily fall into the trap of following a channeler or other type of guru. Discernment is one of the key issues for spiritual healing and spiritual healers, and I hope this book opens up a dialogue about the importance of discernment. Just because something feels good or looks good, it doesn't necessarily mean it is from Spirit.

Today, in my current practice, I continue to work with all kinds of different practitioners – doctors of medicine, eastern disciplines, and numerous healing modalities as will as several psychotherapists – and all work well with energetic healing. I have found this to be a natural fit and mutually beneficial relationship. Unfortunately, our cultural biases present major roadblocks to this type of partnership.

Slowly, bit-by-bit, over the past twenty years or so, people are again beginning to look at the part Spirit plays in our physical lives. Prayer is being encouraged in hospitals because measurable benefits have been recorded in patients who pray or meditate. Science will always prove out healing, just as spiritual healing will always enhance science. That is how it should be. That eliminates ego from both sides.

Chapter Five: My Discovery of Fusion

Of all the practitioners I have worked with, the one with whom I have developed the closest relationship professionally is, of course, Don. The way we began working together evolved gradually and organically. He began to see the enormous benefits of being able to retrain the habits of the mind after I had helped the patient remove the energy of traumas and internal fear, and then doing the homework by processing them in private sessions with their psychotherapist. Don puts it even more simply. He says that the real hook for him is that, when we work together, the client gets a more complete healing.

Working with clients who are currently undergoing psychotherapy, I am often given information that is not intended for me to understand. The information is in a different detail than what I receive working with clients under other circumstances. I just tell the therapists the words I hear, and they interpret them with the client. It is a sort of facilitation of the process, enhancing the psychotherapeutic sessions. All the therapists I work with at this level say it is like adding another very powerful tool to their bag to encourage the person's healing process.

Our Guides always know the right sequence of steps we need to facilitate our healing, the first, second and so on. I am shown the client's basic fears, incidents and resulting cross-wires directly. We release the charge so they can then be opened and explored in therapy. In subsequent sessions, we might revisit issues previously touched upon so we can release them completely. Sometimes we also visit new areas that can open up past hurts in a new light, leading exponentially to more power-packed sessions with their therapist.

It came to me as a surprise that psychotherapy and spiritual healing work well together, as I've been taught that science does not cross over to the spiritual. My Guide taught me that both disciplines are designed to help us deal with our bodies' and souls' reactions to emotional, energetic and spiritual influences. Everything in our environment affects how we think and how we react to each other, and this directly affects the education of the soul. It has been my experience that traditional psychotherapy focuses on the personality, the emotional aspects of the self, and issues associated with "mental illness." When dealing with the psyche, I believe psychotherapists are dealing with the unconscious. I am told by my Guidance -- and my experience has borne it out -- that more than 90 percent of our communication is spiritual and about 10 percent is the conscious and unconscious combined. We all see this played out in daily life: When walking on a street, you feel you are being watched. When the hair goes up on the back of your neck. When you just know who is calling, or when you are walking in a crowded, noisy city and someone you had not noticed and could not hear across the street urgently points to the sky and you react by looking in that direction. This is a gift that helps preserve the somas or life as our soul is communicating with us to stay out of danger. What does law enforcement constantly remind us to do in order to be safe? Trust our instincts!

How interesting would it be if we could tap into this level of existence as a useful and consistent tool? Every client presents in his or her unique paradigm. It is consistent and as individual as a thumbprint.

It is very exciting to hear of the great positive results when an individual accesses this inner wisdom. Then the spiritual aspects of the individual begin to emerge, and this is where the need for a clear and present spiritual healer/medium can be of use.

The knowledge generated by other therapists has indirectly been a part of my soul's education. I say "indirectly" because, as I acknowledged at the outset, my dyslexia prevents me from doing any substantial academic research of my own. I rely on my professional associates to bring me the "textbook" knowledge and debate it with me.

Carl Jung, M. Scott Peck, Joseph Campbell, Malachi Martin, Jean Houston Ph.D., Dr. Daniel J. Benor, Dr. Edward C. Whitmont, Francis MacNutt, and Carolyn Myss Ph.D., have all written about their in-depth observations concerning aspects of the mind, body and soul that can be of help to us. I believe the gifted medium/spiritual healer is the catalyst that joins the healing theories of human experience with the education of the soul for full involvement with the Absolute.

M. Scott Peck, a renowned psychiatrist, has written extensively about his experiences with possessions and exorcisms. Through his work in psychiatry, Peck wrote, he came to know the part of human experience where "normal" explanations and traditional treatment methods were just not enough to explain certain occurrences regarding people's mental stress, nor did these tools provide effective and lasting treatments. Many therapists I talk with also note that modern medical pharmacology treatment can numb just about any symptom, whereas the purpose of psychotherapy and spiritual healing is not to numb anything at all. Our purpose is to uncover and heal whatever ails us, even if that is a "possession," as Peck calls it, or an emotional wound held deep within the unconscious.

It has been my observation that traditional psychotherapy looks at people and their life events and how those events have impacted their learning process and unconscious reactions. Thought processes, beliefs, fears and behaviors seem to be a primary focus. The unconscious world appears to be a significant part of what psychotherapy works with in trying to help the individual resolve problems. For the most part, however, psychotherapy seems to ignore the spiritual and the energetic aspects of human existence. Several therapists have explained to me that Jungian Depth Psychology and dream analysis, Transpersonal Psychology, Humanistic Psychology and Sacred Psychology, to name a few, begin to address these critical aspects of the individual. I do not know this firsthand. However, these discussions have helped me see that others have visited before what I have observed within many clients.

Several therapists have told me that Carl Jung and Joseph Campbell referred to spiritual healers as a necessary part of human existence, but lost to modernization and materialism. What they might have been unable to observe are the "gifts of Healing," because there has been no constant in this area, and so it has not been a scientifically viable method of exploring their theories. It has been our observation that, in order to have a constant, the healer must be a clear and innocent medium with the gifts of seeing, hearing and knowing in order to make observations pertinent and unique to the individual. This is constant information if these parameters are observed. With this powerful tool, such a spiritual healer can easily, innocently and clearly recognize the incidents being observed. This information can then become the starting point on the road map to unlocking the individual's psyche.

Peck also refers to the long and rigorous effort of removing a "demon" from an individual after he had determined that there was, in fact, the presence of "evil." This view is hinted at in many other published views in Peck's field. I am told that Malachi Martin has spent 30 years as a practicing exorcist, and he recounts chilling and dramatic struggles between good and evil, which can damage both the exorcist and the "possessed" person. Many of us have seen the movie *The Exorcist*, a dramatic account of what we have all been taught about exorcism and what many have observed. In research and conversation with other therapists, I have noted how Dr. Peck's and Malachi Martin's experience and vantage point influenced others' understanding of the subject. Because Peck and Malachi recognize how energy affects people, their books offer a potential foundation for the uniting of spirituality and psychiatry in relation to what they acknowledge as possessions.

As a medium/spiritual healer, I can say that this is part of the "missed" information that has been marginalized concerning the "gifts of healing." This process of energy removal is done easily and painlessly in a split second if it is done in the full knowledge and free will of the individual. Only a clear and innocent medium/spiritual healer can easily access the information and the energy to make this transition possible or even plausible. I've often been referred to, as stated earlier, as an "energetic power tool." I am absolutely clear that it is not I, rather the power of Spirit working with me, who is healing and working with the clients. Acting as this energetic power tool is what is called the "gift of command." Once the energy has been identified and understood by the client, and the education of the soul has occurred, the client gives permission, and I simply command the predatory energy to leave. There is no struggle or clash of wills, and the process does not challenge either my faith or the client's, but enhances our faith. The gift of command has nothing to do with performing miracles at will.

It is this misinformation about "miracles" and superhuman struggles that I am trying to correct with this book. In doing so, I hope to highlight the benefits of combining the practices of science and healing. The schism between spirituality and science is outdated and regressive and keeps us from moving forward in our thinking and willingness to explore healing outside the rigid constraints of "modern" society. I have observed that schism as a major contributor to our individual and social stagnation and subsequent social uprisings. If all had access to the equality I see and know, we could and would, sooner or later, have to get along with one another. I believe the spiritual healer/medium is the link that makes this possible.

Colleagues have pointed out to me that both Peck and the School of Spiritual Psychology correctly assert that we need to break down the barriers between science and spirituality. Although I have never studied in the School of Spirituality, I believe the process constitutes spiritual healing rather than Demonology; it seems the natural forum for such healing. My Guidance reminds me that predatory energy is only one part of this discipline, the purpose of which is to heal the human condition and support the education and progression of the soul.   As a species, we should and can be much further along in our energetic and spiritual evolution, but to do so, we need to support people in growing their gifts instead of marginalizing and devaluing them as "freaks." Relegating gifted people to the fringes of society, where they are afraid to even speak of their gifts, let alone grow them and use them to help others, is narrow-minded and of no benefit to them or us. It has the effect of keeping people stuck in the early stages of their gifts. This in turn gives the practice a bad name. It's as if we provided doctors with only one year of medical school and then told them they were on their own from here on out.

Our society has a profound need for a safe and ethical place in which gifted people can learn more about their gifts and how to develop them in order to help others. This training should occur within the ethical boundaries created through the collective discernment and experience of mediums/spiritual healers.

A colleague with whom I enjoy a healthy debate directed me to a web page for a Dr. Daniel J. Benor, a holistic psychiatric psychotherapist and healer and one of a growing band of medical doctors who understand that there is something very natural about combining spiritual healing and psychotherapy. On that site (www.wholistichealingresearch.com) Benor states "Spiritual healing opens people to awareness of deeper meanings to illness, which are then often amenable to psychotherapy. Illness can be a communication from a person's unconscious mind to bring to his awareness various inner conflicts or old hurts that might be ready for release. Illness may be a communication with others, such as a statement of need for love and caring or a protest against stresses. Psychotherapy may then help people to address the root causes of their illnesses."

In her book *Why People Don't Heal and How They Can* (Three Rivers Press, 1998), Carolyn Myss, Ph.D., writes, "When an illness is part of your spiritual journey, no medical intervention can heal you until your spirit has begun to make the changes that the illness was designed to inspire." This is true of spiritual healing as well. I will not be guided to remove energy if the clients don't recognize and understand how that energy got there in the first place and why they might be attached to it, as well as what it might mean to release it from their physical bodies and energy fields. This often requires work in therapy sessions in order to process these issues and educate the somas. It was his reluctance to engage this process that prevented Bob, my former collaborator, from growing his own considerable gifts and relieving himself of his chronic, severe physical problems. If we don't listen to the whispers, Spirit will turn up the volume. It is often said that physical bodies speak to us in metaphor, and illness and injury help the conscious self to pay attention to something we need to understand and heal. Experience has shown me that, if we try to bypass this progression or remove energy before its time, the body or mind will re-manifest a similar if not the same situation again. Sometimes the body will also continue to use the same 'effective' tool to get your attention once the process has begun. I personally have a spot in my back, for example, that flares up if I do not do my own spiritual work. Like everyone else, I am required to depend on others to help me.

A new client invariably asks, "Isn't spiritual healing just like faith healing?" Yes and no. Faith healing requires the subject to believe in a deity of one sort or another, but spiritual healing has no such requirement. Spiritual healing requires the client only to be willing to allow that something might exist beyond our physical grasp. They need to have the desire to understand and work on the underlying causes of their physical ailments. That said, because this world is full of different road maps to the divine in the form of organized religions, it is in these contexts of faith healing that most people hear about "miraculous" cures.

Francis MacNutt, a former Catholic priest and founder of the Christian Healing Ministries in Jacksonville, Florida, provides vivid accounts of physical, emotional and spiritual healing through faith healing and the gift of prayer. His work is grounded in Christianity, and he documents incident after incident of people being healed by the power of the Holy Spirit. Such testimonials are offered by countless other highly educated and respected scientists, both religious and non-religious. This is completely valid, and I embrace all roads to the Absolute. Sadly, some of these cures are only temporary and have, therefore, turned individuals away from their faith communities when, in fact, failure to achieve a lasting healing was merely the inability to identify deeper learning that was required. Instead of alienating, such healing experiences that fall short of our expectations should inspire us to move forward in the search for a process more effective for the particular individual. We need to say to ourselves: I received relief during a spiritual session of some sort, so there is something beyond the physical. Now I need to keep searching! Unfortunately most do not have this "searching" frame of reference.

The kind of spiritual healing services I provide have been documented for ages. I do not call any of this "new age." We have all read the bible story in which Jesus Christ cures a woman of her emotional and physical ailments and then says to her, "Go and sin no more." Spiritual healing services are, in fact, the "go and sin no more" part. The problems identified by the medium/spiritual healer are processed and learned from so we can "go and sin no more," thereby changing the damaging behavior.

Unfortunately these experiences have been downgraded to the realms of fringe religious beliefs, quirky alternative medicines, or ancient, outdated cultures. Running through the vast majority of literature on the subject is a common thread that attempts to diminish, devalue and discredit spiritual healing. I believe this is because there is no safe place to fully explore and develop the gifts of healing, creating an atmosphere devoid of ethics and education and so, filled with shame. I fully recognize that these attitudes are grounded in fear of the unknown. I have no illusions about how this book will be received by many people who have been influenced by such fear. That explains my reservations about writing the book. Hopefully, however, I can encourage at least a few to turn toward research and debate.

When I am working on a client who exhibits certain physical symptoms, I am often shown the incident that caused the energetic block now manifesting as those symptoms. In the early days of my practice, I simply released the energy from that incident, believing that would allow the body to cure the physical problems. And it does, but only in the short term. I noticed clients returning with a recurrence of the same symptoms and a buildup of energy around the same issues, much like what we often hear about with faith healing – temporary solutions.

One session in which a client had returned with recurring symptoms led to my collaboration with psychotherapists. During this session I was shown a therapist's face. That's about as clear a clue as one can get, I suppose; even I was able to interpret it. So I sent the client to the professional to do his "homework" regarding his psychological and emotional processing of the incident that I was being shown, the apparent underlying cause of his problems. In that psychotherapy, the client was able to gain insight and understanding of his issues, enabling him to "let go" of the incident. This, in turn, provided significant emotional relief and the avenue for a permanent release of the physical manifestations of the incident and its energetic root during his next spiritual healing session. That interim step allowed for permanent healing in a session with me! The psychotherapist and I were both amazed and encouraged that something new and exciting had just occurred.

Working together, psychotherapists and I have found that both the psychological and the spiritual healings of our clients are deeper and more profound than when we work separately, and the overall healing process of the individual moves along much more quickly. In other words, the clients get a bigger bang for their buck. We have found this to be consistent with all who engage in the dual-therapy process.

An outstanding example of how psychotherapy and spiritual healing work better together than separately occurred a few years ago when a middle-aged woman came to see me on a referral from her psychotherapist. Helen had been in therapy for several years and just wasn't making progress, so her therapist, who knew of my work, thought I might be able to help.

During my meditation on Helen before our appointment, I was told very clearly by my Guides that Helen's therapist had to attend her healing session. They had never requested anything like this before, but the therapist was perfectly willing and so was present when I began to work on Helen. As I tapped into her energy, I was shown such horrific scenes from her life that I will not describe them here. Suffice it to say that what I saw was so awful it brought tears to my eyes and I had to look away from Helen so she wouldn't see.

I was guided to ask Helen a few simple questions and then simply wait quietly as the Guides began to give Helen answers. Gradually, the horrible truth of her life, which she had been blocking out for over fifty years, was revealed to her. As this unthinkable information began to flood back into Helen's memory, she began to wail in excruciating emotional pain. At that point, her therapist stepped in and began to work with her in what I can only describe as a crisis intervention. Together, we were able to stabilize Helen energetically and psychologically, and by the end of the session she said she actually felt a little better.

Her therapist maintained daily contact with Helen over the next few weeks as she worked through the psychological effects of what had been revealed in her session. A few months later I received a wonderful note from Helen, letting me know how much she appreciated my working with her. She said it had given her a whole new lease on life. Helen had been stuck in her stagnant situation for nearly thirty years. It was quite apparent to me that, without the involvement of her psychotherapist at the time of her session with me, Helen's breakthrough healing progress would not have occurred.

Psychotherapy and spiritual healing seem to form a more complete therapeutic tool for the whole person. No aspect of the individual is left out. And it is not only the clients who benefit from this relationship but both the healer and the therapist. If the two practitioners are open and willing, they can learn and grow their gifts through such collaboration. A very intuitive therapist I know says she has gained confidence in her gifts of knowing through working with me and by seeing the manifestations of what she just "knew" come true in a safe, nurturing environment. Clients now frequently say to her, "How did you know that?" to which she replies confidently, "It's what I'm being given."

Chapter Six: Terms and Concepts Defined

In his book, *The Mountain of Silence: A Search for Orthodox Spirituality* (Image, 2002), Kyriacos C. Markides offers this incisive dialogue concerning the way to know God:

"If we, therefore, wish to explore and get to know God, it would be a gross error to do so through our senses or with telescopes, seeking Him out in outer space.

Can we then conclude that for modern, rational human beings, metaphysical philosophy like that of Plato and Aristotle or rational theology is the appropriate method?

It would be equally foolish and naive to seek God with our intellect... Consider it axiomatic that God cannot be investigated through such approaches.

So, Platonic and Aristotelian metaphysics are not the way to know God.

But of course not. That's the language given to us by all the elders and saints throughout history. Logic and reason cannot investigate and know that which is beyond logic and reason.

That's what the mystics have been saying time and again. That God cannot be talked about but must be experienced. But what does that mean? Does it mean that God cannot be studied?

No. We can and must study God, and we can reach God and get to know Him.

But how?

Christ Himself revealed to us the method. He told us that not only are we capable of exploring God, but we can also live with Him, become one with Him. And the organ by which we can achieve that is neither our senses nor our logic but our hearts."

Now you have followed me on my journey to becoming a spiritual healer. Along the way, I have introduced a number of concepts and terms that can be a little confusing. My own story has little value unless you understand what spiritual healing is all about, so, at this point, I will offer my best explanation for the key terms and concepts. Let's look at Spirit, or the Absolute, first.

What is Spirit/The Absolute?

Not a man of great eloquence, I thought I had better get some help with this one, so I meditated on the question and this is the response I got from my Guides.

Spirit, or the Absolute, as I like to call it, is the life of the universe, the knowledge and thoughts that connect us all and connect all of our souls. It is neither male nor female, because it is not biological. It is what exists beyond the physical life force. Spirit is curious about the physical world because the physical world is constantly changing. That is what makes it infinite. Spirit is too big to exist within biological beings, which are delicate and finite, but Spirit is the force, or glue, that holds us all together. It is the driving force of biological evolution and the reason for it. Spirit is the foundation for the finite, and the basis of the infinite. It is not one; it is all, so it cannot be defined through a biological thought or definition.

Bit of a mouthful, right? Yes, it can sound a little complicated and intimidating, but that is only if you try to comprehend it in human terms. Don't. You will fail. Instead, allow for the possibilities outside the confines of what you've been taught. In order to experience the Absolute, or to have a partnership with it (a life of prayer or meditation), you must find the strength of self-worth to allow the Absolute into your heart. Spirit is not intellectual. If you like, you can think of Spirit as the energy of everything. That's about as simply as I can put it.

How Spirit/the Absolute Works

Spirit is the thread of commonality. All is reflected in each. That is why biological vessels of learning (humans) are so similar. The biological is so fragile and finite that it cannot live long enough to learn fully, so it is replicated, providing numerous learning opportunities. Spirit requires many of the same types of vessels over and over again to continue seeking knowledge, to continue the infinite, to experience love, biological urges and needs such as touch and emotion: the joy of birth, the pain of death, and the entire physical experience

The entire physical experience cannot mature without strife -- biological and spiritual grist, if you will. And nothing can mature in an unbiased way without free will. So, full knowledge cannot be achieved without free will. The Holy Spirit is the protector of free will, the protector of the biological life force for the ever-expanding Absolute. Without the Absolute, there would be no purpose for the biological to exist. The Holy Spirit balances the biological and the individual spirit to create an innocent learning vessel with free will for the growth of individual spirituality. It is the dynamic, or working, hand of the Absolute. Spirit is the force that can be drawn on for this ultimate cause and direction, and it will do what is necessary to maintain and secure the purpose of life and free will.

The Absolute is the reason for all biological and spiritual unions, i.e. life. We are all interconnected by this common origin, and because Spirit is essentially everything, we are all interdependent. That is why one person's learning or one person's struggle affects the community: We all share the same energy. We are also similar because we share the same type of classroom, which is the physical body. The physical body is our learning tool. But, although Spirit connects everyone and everything, we are all a little bit different. God, or the Absolute, made it that way. Since everyone is different genetically, the species has to keep learning and growing. That is evolution. And that's perfect, because the fact that Spirit can work through diversity and change is what makes Spirit omnipotent, constantly growing and constantly knowing. It attains knowledge at the time of that new growth. That is perfection.

The Physical (or the Body)
The energy of that which is already created is the biological and molecular energy of the planets, the sun, the universe, etc. It is chemical and biological. It has a force, or energy, that can be measured and seen. The physical is the vessel for the beginning of learning, or for life. When the earth was raw, it had everything necessary to create life. That is an aspect of creation. At this point, the molecules could come together to make the life-force energy of non-animals: rocks, plants and

trees. Then, the energy of animals, or carbon-based life, could evolve until the proper vessel for learning was created – us. As our bodies evolved, they could tolerate the higher soul unions that separate us from the animals and make us human: Adam and Eve provide a simplistic example. A "higher soul union" means that, as the body genetically evolved into a more advanced state with larger brain capacity, the species was able to handle a soul that vibrates at a higher frequency, creating what we call humans. In contrast, if an evolved soul were to enter a dog, for example, that soul would simply remain stagnant.

The human body has four imperatives: the need to survive, the need to procreate, the need to do no harm to other humans, and the drive to learn. These are the reasons for the biological existence of a body, and they create the will of the human body, which means, of course, that the physical body does have a will of its own. Thus, when one human hurts another human, there's an adrenaline rush because we're going against the natural will of the body. Some people are addicted to that rush, and they become murderers. Often, they start out killing animals and then they work up to human beings. Other people seek that adrenaline rush through much more benign activities like bungee jumping or sky diving.

The physical body has an involuntary nervous system, which is a learning tool, much like the brain. It holds onto energy in order to keep us safe and help us learn, such as when we learn not to touch things that are hot. This system has a physical memory that can be felt and measured. It affects how our bodies grow. You've probably noticed someone with a hunched or protective posture that may have been developed by cowering before abusive parents. When I look into a person's physical body, I am shown these "incidents of learning." They may present as damaged organs or joints or any other type of physical ailment. This is some of the energy I work with that often results in physical healing, if that is what is intended.

Our bodies consist of three distinct but interrelated aspects: the physical body, the psychic body and the noetic body. An "energy field" called the etheric membrane, which holds us together on all levels of our existence, surrounds each of these three aspects. And just to confuse matters further, etheric energy also comes in two flavors, the etheric membrane, as discussed, and the etheric body, which is a reflection of the physical body. Within these are many sub-systems that I will not attempt to discuss now; semantics could make this long and arduous. Together, I call this the etheric system, which encompasses our complete existence in all its forms. It is the etheric system that allows us to experience all the non-physical aspects of existence such as astral travel, deja vu, premonitions and more while maintaining our energetic integrity. Let me see if I can clarify these descriptions for you.

The psychic body and the noetic body are actually the two parts that comprise our noetic system. When we extend ourselves into non-physical realms, it is the noetic system that extends and the etheric system that holds it together to maintain individual energetic boundaries. In simple terms, the etheric body attaches the physical to the spiritual, all the way down to the space between our atoms. I am often directed to work with the etheric body in healing sessions to manipulate a client's physical tissues, thereby affecting a "cure" or physical healing, such as mending a broken bone.

All of these bodies and systems exist simultaneously and work together to produce the full you. And just to be clear, some of these terms that I use have been coined by others merely to try to explain things in a way we, as humans, can comprehend. Other people may use different terminology for describing the same things. Part of the reason I'm writing this book is to create a common language which we can all understand and use. A common language will help unite us in understanding and bring spiritual healing back into the mainstream of our culture, where it belongs.

So, our lives have three aspects of existence: the physical body; the noetic system, which comprises the psychic body and the noetic body; and the etheric system, which comprises the etheric body and the etheric membranes surrounding each of the bodies.

The physical body is that which you are most familiar with. It is the skin and bones, the organs, muscles and tissues. The physical body wears out after a period of time, but that is only because it is organic and biodegradable. When the physical body "dies," the person's life force or energy remains intact. The noetic and etheric systems continue on for the purpose of learning.

The physical body creates biological energy in many forms, not only the obvious ones when we generate motion or body heat, but even biochemical, electrical energy, such as that created when we think a thought. This energy, or thought form, can be projected consciously or unconsciously, and these thought forms, in essence, do not fade with time. One of the terms coined for these thought forms is "elementals."

In her reading and research for me, a therapist and close colleague found this clear explanation by Markides: *"Any feeling or any thought that an individual projects is an elemental. They have shape and a life of their own, independent of the one who projected them. ... Once these elementals are thrust outwards, they have a shape and existence of their own. Elementals, therefore, can affect others who vibrate on the same frequency as the person or persons who projected them. A Researcher of Truth must, through self-analysis and appropriate meditation exercises, project only benign elementals that can be of help to others."* – **The Magus of Strovolos: The Extraordinary World of a Spiritual Healer** by Kyriacos C. Markides. (Penguin Nonclassics, 1989).

Markides, a professor at the University of Maine who has devoted his life to the study of the sociology of religion, non-medical healing (spiritual healing) and Christian Mysticism, has written several books about Spyros Sathi (affectionately known as Daskalos, which means teacher) and Kostas, two spiritual healers from Markides' native island of Cyprus, and other works on the nature of spirituality. He states, "One is always linked to be accountable for the elementals that one ceaselessly creates." That is the way the laws of cause and effect work.

Our thoughts create energy and, as such, they have mass. It is our intention that moves this energy. We call these "thought forms" elementals. This is why it is so important for us to be aware of and responsible for our own thoughts. This phenomenon is the Absolute's way of making us collectively learn from our experiences. In fact, I have enabled many of my clients to actually feel the heat or the cold energy of their elementals. For example, you may have seen a cheery, outgoing, positive individual start work in an office full of miserable, unhappy people, and the person very quickly become like them. That is the effect of the group's elementals acting upon the individual. Many people call this simply "negative energy." A better term might be that other popular phrase, "negative vibe." "Vibe" is short for vibration, and that is a more accurate description of these elementals, as they are a form of energy that vibrates at different frequencies, causing different effects. You may also have experienced how, when you are in a great mood, things around you just start going your way, and others react toward you in a positive manner. That is the effect of your elementals, or positive vibe, on others. Markides warns that we have to be careful to project only "benign elementals that can be of help to others."

All animals create elementals – dogs, cats, snakes, rabbits, giraffes and humans – but humans are the worst. This constitutes indiscriminate energy that we are, in fact, responsible for, and it affects us all. Elemental energy is the reason we feel different in a mall than we do at home, in the office or the forest. This plethora of elemental energy that we are constantly creating generates spiritual static, which is why I am directed to clear my clients' basic energy fields before I work on them. If I don't do so, when I get into a client's energy field, I hear all the noise from these elementals. I call this "incidental energy." Most of it has no learning value for the client, so those parts need to be removed; otherwise we could get bogged down in a lot of insignificant activity in addressing this energy.

In a process I call "energy reclamation," I teach my clients to pull back any of the energy, or elementals, they have given off or lost that are, in fact, learning tools. When clients do this over a period of time, they begin to feel like their old selves again. In order for a full healing to take place, they need to pull back the energy of these elementals so they can learn from them. During this energy reclamation, they can also pull back the energy that someone has taken from them in a predatory way, such as when a narcissistic or aggressive person has made them feel bad. This energy transfer is one of the things we have to balance; taking back our elementals is a valuable learning experience.

The etheric body is the reflection of the physical. It is the sum total of the life force of all our organs and every cell memory of our tissue. It shows trauma, health and vitality, or lack thereof, for every aspect of the physical body. It is the part that tells us when something is wrong physically, or about to go wrong, such as when the hairs on the back of your neck stand up, or when you get what I like to call the "psychic shiver." It is the extended nervous system of the physical body, giving us intuitive feelings. The etheric body gives us foreknowledge for safety and health. It is also where I see disease. When I view the etheric body, it is like seeing one of those plastic models of a human's physiology that are used in science class, from which you can take out each organ and look at it. Similarly, when the Guides direct me to a part of the body in a client that has a problem, we can lift out that etheric organ, turn it around and give it a thorough examination.

The noetic body has been described as the "body of thoughts." It is the sum total of all of our learning through the emotions, thoughts and occurrences experienced by the physical body in this life. It consists of the inner chakra, the physical chakra and the spiritual chakra. I don't believe anyone has made this distinction between the physical, spiritual and inner chakras before. This is something I have learned as I've grown in experience as a spiritual healer. My Guides show me more and more as I progress. I am frequently called upon to use all three levels of the chakra system in order to fully help clients, which lead us rather neatly to:

The Chakra System

How do all these different aspects of our existence work together – the two aspects of Spirit and the three aspects of the body? This is where chakras come in, which I describe as the windows on our learning system or the points of contact between the etheric and physical bodies and the noetic system. Webster's provides a more clinical definition: "Any of the points of spiritual power located along the body." The study and explanation of the many chakras already fills a library, so I will limit this discussion to a brief overview of the seven main chakras.

First Chakra

The first chakra is located between the base of the pelvis and the knees and expands its influence below our feet. This is the first point of contact as we come into our physical bodies. It shows the seer the immediate health of the body and how the individual's early life, archetypes etc. affect his/her intrinsic points of view in this life.

This chakra has been referred to as our root chakra, in that, if operating correctly, it allows our soul to expand to about three feet below our feet. When the first chakra is expanded, we are in full contact with the earth and its molecular energy, which has been referred to in the New Age movement and Eastern philosophies as "being grounded."

It is the anchoring and ending point for the Kundalini, or cord that connects the chakras. It is not the beginning. The Kundalini reaches the first chakra as the individual opens up to the power of God, or Spirit. If the Kundalini appears to open here, the individual has artificially, through hallucinogenic drugs or other means, tried to bypass the natural progression of the soul. This is done to seek power at the human level. (These attempts open the soul only to predatory energy. Spirit cannot be forced.)

The first chakra shows the seer a person's ability to trust, feel secure and take care of him or herself. From that, the ability for prosperity, survival and physical health can be seen. It shows the ability to be grounded and satisfied. It also shows the seer things that have happened in a person's life that have not already been processed energetically and physically, and reveals any opportunities that occurred for learning prior to that physical life.

Second Chakra

The second chakra is located between the pelvis and navel. It contains the hips, pelvis, sexual organs, lower small intestines, appendix, bladder, kidneys (which also have a special connection to the third chakra), lower back, and the nerves feeding the legs, as well as all the muscles and other tissues thereof.

This chakra shows the seer how you relate to the world. It is the center of your physical power. If it is weak we do not, and cannot, have successful personal relationships. If all is healthy, it shows the seer your ability to receive and give pleasure sexually as well as emotionally.

It is where we hold the interaction of all human relationships, including guilt, frustration, loving openness, all meaningful exchanges, as well as love of self and self-gratification and the willingness to feel emotions and accept changes.

The second chakra shows the seer what has been left energetically and physically unprocessed within that person's life during mid-childhood to the present.

Third Chakra

The third chakra spans from the navel to the diaphragm. It contains most of the large intestine, stomach, pancreas, liver, gallbladder, spleen, kidneys and spinal cord, and all the tissues thereof.

This is where we get our personal physical strength. If this area is compromised, our nutrition is out of balance and we are physically weak. This area is also where one can gather personal energy and manipulate it. It can be moved to various parts of the body to promote a certain amount of physical healing.

The energy of the third chakra is what others perceive from us when we walk into a room. It is our charisma, our personal power, basically a nonverbal exchange of energy. If the energy of this chakra is healthy, we are liked and have vitality, spontaneity and purpose, as well as balance and self-esteem. It indicates we're not frozen in fear; we act appropriately and are willing to risk being wrong in any given situation.

It indicates a person who can have non-dominating power and autonomy, thereby making him or her effective.

Fourth Chakra

The fourth chakra is located from the diaphragm to roughly the collarbone. It is known as the heart chakra, as it contains the heart and lungs, spinal cord and tissues thereof.

This is a much misinterpreted chakra. It is the center of our spiritual strength, the point at which our spiritual energy, physical energy and energy from creation come together. Unfortunately, we have been taught to give away energy from this area. When we "give from the heart" it is a very personal donation and should be exchanged only for equally personal energy, such as in a marriage or other intimate personal relationship in which the energetic exchanges are equal on all levels: physically, emotionally and spiritually. In any relationship that is not an equal exchange, we become personally insulted, angry and frustrated, and emotionally, physically and mentally depleted. When this happens, the energy flow to the physical body becomes very weak, followed by compromises to our physical health.

If healthy, this chakra shows the seer a person's ability to give and receive deep love and compassion. The client appears to have a good sense of peace and centeredness.

If the individual acknowledges the presence of Spirit, the chakra brightens and Spirit causes us to relax and display vitality, self-confidence and contentment of self and our relationship to the divine.

Fifth Chakra

The fifth chakra runs from our collarbones through our sinuses. It includes the thyroid, all of the throat and neck, mouth, ears, shoulders, arms and hands, and all the tissues thereof.

This is the most volatile of all our chakras. It is where we speak and search for our truth. If we do not speak and search for our truth, the chakra is weakened and can shut off, cutting off the supply of spiritual energy to the rest of the body.

Why did Spirit make this chakra so sensitive? To make us exchange information so we can search, grow and learn in order to complete our spiritual purpose. We are made as social creatures. If we do not socialize, there is something wrong. Socializing does not mean that you have to be the life of the party, but rather it is the exchange of energy through ideas, ideals and/or creations of any sort that express where we are, what we are interested in, what we are searching for and, thereby, who we are to become.

The fifth chakra is for communication, creativity and productivity. It is for communication through vibration as well as touch, and has a direct connection to sight. It shows the seer the ability of people to communicate their true selves, whether they know it or not, as well as showing the development of their verbal and nonverbal abilities to communicate.

Sixth Chakra

The sixth chakra is our brain and our nervous system, which includes a connection to our five senses. It is the mechanism that gathers information for the conscious and unconscious mind.

This is the point where Spirit gives us information. It is where all of our spiritual gifts manifest themselves. People who use their gifts on a regular basis actually develop larger pituitary glands than those who do not. The pituitary gland is located directly behind the pineal gland in the brain, directly between your eyes; hence it is often referred to as the "third eye." The pituitary gland is also the point where the sixth chakra connects to the seventh chakra.

Spirit uses our senses to communicate the knowledge necessary to use our gifts. This sensing has been labeled clairvoyance (inner vision), clairsentience (inner knowing and feeling), and clairaudience (inner hearing).

Spirit uses the unique experiences of each seer to communicate to us. That is why every person's gifts manifest from a different point of view. This is why we need to work in groups and use the fifth and sixth chakras together to clarify and discern information.

If this chakra is healthy, it shows the seer that the person can place herself with others in all situations, as well as in the grand design of God. The use of this chakra is considered in Western tradition as pathological, because people who use it are sometimes considered insane. In Native American and Eastern traditions it is seen as a necessary gift for spiritual growth.

Seventh Chakra

The seventh chakra, or crown chakra, is purely spiritual, connecting the physical body with the spiritual realms. It is connected to the pituitary gland by the Kundalini, but does not have physical energy within it.

This chakra expands like a funnel to about a foot or more above the head and is our direct line to Spirit. It contains the beginnings of the tunnel that people report seeing when they have a near-death experience. It is, in fact, a tube that is a protected area, which leads through to the divine. It is a road of sorts, upon which we communicate and travel. Upon death, not near-death, our soul energy travels up this cord and it closes behind us, never to return to that body.

This is the place where we all can move to communicate with angels or Guides. When we meditate and find the space of peace, it is, in fact, the soul moving up this cord away from the noise of the planet. It is a very relaxing and enjoyable experience, assuming this chakra and cord have not been compromised. If the cord has been compromised or polluted, the mediator will find it very difficult, if not impossible, to reach this place of peaceful existence.

The cord, or Kundalini, reaches through all of the chakras like a bridge, down to the first, so that the Absolute can nourish, replenish and cleanse us physically and spiritually. Its anchor resides between the first and second chakras, near the sacral. This chakra shows the seer an individual's spiritual connection to the Absolute.

When I look at a chakra, it appears like a series of rings making up a spinning disk, kind of like a CD. Each ring can indicate issues within that person that need to be dealt with. I also see what I refer to as "inner" chakras, which look like a series of circular lights. The best way I can describe one is that it looks a little like a wormhole, as shown in science fiction movies. The inner chakras tend to contain a person's baggage, or the debris of incidents in that person's life.

When I am working on a client, the Guides direct me to look into whichever chakra needs addressing first. So I look into that chakra's "disk" and see something on that disk knocking it out of balance and slowing it down, as if a weight has been added to one side. Generally I see two aspects of the chakras, the physical and the spiritual, and sometimes they are spinning together in perfect alignment (a healthy chakra), and sometimes they are separated. There is always a reason when they are apart. When someone's spirit is apart from his physical, I may say he is "beside himself," because that's exactly how it looks to me.

Usually, if one of the chakras is out of alignment, it throws the others out as well, much like one cog spinning out of line in a machine will cause the whole thing to go out of balance and break down. This noetic system goes out of alignment when the individual has learning to do. Once the learning has taken place, the chakras balance themselves. If they have to be manipulated into balance by outside energy, then the learning is not complete and the imbalance will recur. When there is a significant imbalance, the soul will move aside and you will feel "beside yourself." This is our "noetic warning system" in action.

When I see that, I will first ask why it is happening – I never assume anything – and the Guides will start showing me pictures. They use pictures a lot because words are very limiting. A quick sequence of pictures can convey a complex situation that would be very difficult to describe in a few words. Even so, I sometimes just don't get it, so I ask for another picture (Hey, I'm only human) and we'll banter back and forth until they have got the message through my thick skull. Once we've balanced one chakra, we'll go on to the next, and sometimes we go back and forth because they are all interrelated and/or connected by the energetic pathways.

Some people say the Kundalini resides at the back of the second chakra, but I "see" and observe that is not strictly accurate. It is the cord that shares energy between the physical chakras, if everything is balanced. If everything is not balanced and/or the energy cord is forced into activity by drug use with intent or prolonged meditations, I have seen that the individual can be damaged. This can be a warning sign, for me, that something is directly affecting their physical well being. This energy will then remain open between the second and third chakra until the damage is repaired. If it is not, it can forever alter one's personality and undermine the healthy functioning of the chakra system and the physical body.

Angels, Guides and Messengers

Angels and Guides are almost the same things. Guides can have existed in the physical body before, whereas what we term an "angel" has never, and can never, be in physical form. Angels were not meant to be physical. What is sometimes called a "messenger" is just a different type of angel, again, one that does not have prolonged contact with a physical body.

"Angel" is very much a Judeo-Christian term, but in the interests of simplicity I will continue to use it. We think of angels as having wings, but both angels and Guides are energetic beings and have no specific form. They are energy, just like our soul. They can take on any guise whatsoever in order to fit within our mental understanding and constructs. They put on a face for us only because the biological mind is so finite and fragile that it has to have something to relate to. This is also why energy will show itself differently to different people and why discernment is so important.

For me, angels and Guides often first manifest as a color, which is a vibration, of course. Each color vibrates at a different frequency: the higher the frequency, the lighter the color. Thus, orange vibrates at a much higher frequency than black. Consequently, when I see angels and Guides, I can tell by looking at their colors which energetic states they are projecting, such as peace, joy, wisdom, trust, or tenderness etc.. These energetic beings also fulfill various important needs for us in our lives, which correspond to their colors and their vibrations. For example, one of my Guides is primarily pink and vibrates at an empathetic and loving level. This is often what clients feel during a session, which gives them a greater sense of safety and trust. It's like when you walk into a home where cookies are baking and the smell gives you a warm, cozy feeling. There is a correlation between the vibration of the energetic being, the color and the need it fulfills for people. These vibrations influence our noetic system the same way that scent influences our nervous system. They perfume our essence.

These angels, Guides and messengers, or energetic beings, all communicate with us symbolically, much as if in our dreams. I have agreed upon the meanings of a number of symbols with the angels and Guides I communicate with regularly in order to make it easier for me to understand what they are trying to tell me. However, when I'm working with a client's Guides, if we don't have that common frame of reference, I might have to ask my Guides to interpret for me.   So now that we have explored these various definitions, let's try and put them all into the context of the spiritual healing practice. We'll use Charlene as an example.

Charlene was a client I worked on with Don. During my pre-session meditation, my Guides showed me images in all of her chakras, but for the purpose of this example I am going to concentrate on what they showed me in her fourth, or heart, chakra.

The Guides showed me that the right side of Charlene's heart was dark and ill, containing a great deal of unhealthy energy. Then they showed me the image of a hot air balloon hovering above the fourth chakra with a lifeline connecting down into her heart. This balloon represented God, who was providing a lifeline to Charlene's physical heart because it was in such bad shape. The Guides continued with the images by showing me an anguished young girl who had a lot of unacknowledged fear, sadness and anger.

Next they began to run a series of "movies" for me, each one showing a facet of Charlene's broken heart, incidents in her past that had hurt her. I was also shown how she was keeping the stories current because she thought it would keep her safe. She developed a habit of requiring herself to see her wounds from her young child's point of view. In other words, she kept replaying these stories in her mind over and over again, both consciously and unconsciously.

At the healing session, the Guides directed me to start work on the heart chakra first, as that was the one in the worst condition, as was her physical heart. I was shown the symbol of an elephant, which, according to my agreed-upon symbols, represents an inability to learn new things and a susceptibility to be hurt when people did not understand her. I was instructed to remove the elephant, or energy, which I did.

Then the Guides informed me that Charlene's issues began when her father beat her for telling the truth. Charlene confirmed that had happened to her a lot at a young age. I was shown a piece of her soul that had been relegated to a "cave" in her heart, and the Guides brought this soul piece from her childhood back and integrated it into her current consciousness and into her current physical heart, as well as into her current fourth chakra. The Guides impressed upon Charlene that she needed to know people would listen to her and believe her. They also showed me that this piece of her soul from her childhood was surrounded by a lot of color, which indicated a lot of spiritual protection. When we are involved with traumatic incidents throughout our life, we face a steep learning curve. The fact that these happenings are dramatic makes them difficult to learn from at the moment, but learn we must! To remind the conscious mind that we have work to do, the soul fragments, meaning a small piece of us moves away from the main energy pattern. This is much like a scab on the physical body reminding us to be careful. This fragment functions as an irritant to remind the unconscious that we are not whole or that our boundaries have been violated, spurring us on to learn what actually happened earlier in our lives. Unfortunately we do not use this information on a daily basis. If we did, we would quickly seek out the reason this warning system is activated, such as when we are uncomfortable with certain people but not with others.

Once that was completed, there was a large hole in the physical heart underneath the symbol of her young child, which was repaired energetically by the Guides. They "fixed" a muscle in the top right-hand corner of the heart and then proceeded to "remove" a good degree of debris from her arteries.

I then saw an image of a ball, along with a garden fairy and a frog, all representations of predatory energy within her heart that were trying to get at that piece of her soul that was hiding in the cave in her heart. In this case, the frog represented death, and so, with the client's permission and understanding of her issues, I was able to remove that energy.

As you can see, it is a step-by-step process. First I am shown one thing and I deal with it, then I am shown the next thing to work on, etc. The next energy I dealt with manifested as a large worm, which I pulled out through her right ear. After that, I saw a nightingale that was smashed into Charlene's heart. This was representative of her inspiration, talents, joy and music, all of which she knew she had, but she had been unable to enjoy them during her adult life. I healed this energy and incorporated it into her physical heart as well as her heart chakra.

Based upon all the information we gleaned from this session, Don was then able to help Charlene, in subsequent therapy sessions, continue to process the initial incident of her father beating her. As we have discussed before, it is essential to process in order for the healings I perform to be complete so the symptoms do not re-manifest. It was this original incident that taught Charlene not to trust her own truth, or anyone else's, especially people of authority. Because most of the energy from this incident had been removed in the healing session, the lifelong habits Charlene had formed because of it were much more amenable to the psychotherapeutic process.

It is very important for me to underscore the fact that I learned everything I'm writing about on my own, through direct guidance from Spirit. The words came later. I am just one guy, living my life the best way I can, and developing a profound trust in my relationship with the Absolute. Most of this occurred quietly, privately, without the benefit of a spiritual mentor or teacher. I had no one to talk with or to help me create a frame of reference for what was happening to me. I have the gift of dyslexia, which limits my reading and, therefore, my research of other spiritual healers, but this gift set me up for the experience of blind faith and a very direct relationship with my Guides. This created a classroom of innocent trust, where I am constantly being taught and developed as a spiritual healer.

I have learned that words and constructs are not as important as what is happening in the healing session. This is faith. I have to trust the Absolute, beyond semantics, in order to do what is right. There are many different belief systems, each with its unique semantics, that have served to subvert and marginalize spiritual healing because there has been no common language developed to discuss it. While I believe the Absolute is unknowable, within each of us is an innocent seeker with the innate ability to connect with divine guidance. Each view can be a piece in the development of this language. I am not trying to define the boundaries. I am trying to develop a common language for the benefit of creating a cohesive body of knowledge for spiritual healing.

As a child, I was taught to go before God in innocence, and it is this innocence that keeps us from getting in our own way. I haven't been able to focus on developing the specific mechanics of spiritual healing. Rather, my life has been a very experiential journey with my Guides. It is important for you to understand this because the same truth exists for you. We all have the ability to come to our Guides and learn through direct, innocent experience. If you take away nothing else from this book, please know this.

Chapter Seven: The Healer's Toolbox

As we come to the end of this journey through my spiritual awakening and my road to becoming a spiritual healer, I recognize that there are still many questions left unanswered. Although it would be impossible to address every one of those questions in a single book (at least not one that can be carried by one person!) I do want to discuss some of the most obvious and important issues, such as what healers are and are not; the nature of evil; the importance of discernment; and the role of faith and innocence.

But first we need to get something out of the way, and that something is a little item called "language."

Overcoming Language Barriers

Language has been a barrier to understanding since humankind uttered its first grunt. One man's "Ugh" is another man's "Ugh?" The creation of different languages for different regions only compounded the problem and contributed to the suspicion and hostility that still exist between nations and pathways to the divine.

Spiritual healing is not exempt from these problems, far from it. In fact, even within one language, English, there are so many different terms and explanations for the same things that anyone trying to study the subject could be forgiven for thinking that no one knows what they are talking about. Therefore, it is important to break down the barriers to our understanding of spiritual healing that have been caused by language. The terms and descriptions we have used in this book might not be the most commonly accepted; however, they could form the foundation for a new dialogue between psychology and spirituality, the individual and the Absolute.

As previously discussed, thoughts create energy, and it is our language that forms our thoughts. Therefore, language has been part of our energetic experience from its inception. This is why language is so important to our experience and understanding. Language provides a tool to help us generate the beginning of an understanding of the Absolute and to allow for the possibilities of an existence beyond our own physical experience, but, because it is susceptible to ego, it can and is also used to manipulate thoughts and experiences.

Since its creation, language has been used to control people, which is why it is so important to demystify and deconstruct ancient preconceptions. Humans interpret everything they hear and read through their own filters, experience and agendas, so we need to question in order to get to the truth of our beliefs and to a thorough understanding. Language has structured and restricted our experience of the Absolute, but it is only our personal experience and relationship with the Absolute that has truth and meaning. That authentic experience is a knowing.

Access to language has historically been the territory of the prevailing institutions and a universally accepted tool for education. Education provides knowledge, and knowledge, as they say, is power, which is why so many religions and political institutions have sought to restrict the education of women, slaves and commoners alike. It is this restriction of knowledge that has cast a shadow on spiritual healing in general. However, true spiritual healing cannot be controlled by language, theories or human agendas. Perhaps this is why it is so threatening to so many.

If it helps, try not to think of any of the words we use throughout this book as authoritative. When we refer to the Absolute, some of you may prefer to think of the word "God" or "Allah" or "Jehovah" or perhaps "universal truth" or "perfection." At the end of the day, we each have our own way of addressing the Absolute. We also refer to the "Holy Spirit," or "Spirit," as the working hand of God/the Absolute. How we humans name something does not change the nature of that thing, so we should not allow any differences in semantics to separate us, as they have done for centuries. Instead, allow yourself to find the Absolute that resides within you; it is not bound by cultures, religions or language. You will surprise yourself in discovering just how much knowledge you already have inside you if you give it the opportunity to come out. Sadly, we humans will continue to obscure discernment until we can, once again, individually find that place of innocence which is free of the uneducated ego.

In his book *Homage to the Sun: the Wisdom of the Magus of Strovolos* (Arkana, 1987), Kyriacos C. Markides writes about something Daskalos said: "What did Christ say? 'Blessed be the meek in spirit.' By that he did not mean the fools and idiots, as some naively assumed, but those who are innocent of slyness and knavery. It is neither cleverness nor the accumulation of knowledge that will lead us to self-realization, but a clean heart. 'Blessed be the pure at heart,' He said, 'for they shall see God.'"

For example, does it feel right that God would create a wonderfully diverse race of humans only to see the vast majority of us automatically damned to hell just because we do not follow the "one true religion"?

Does it feel right that our Creator would single out any one nation or race as superior?

Does it feel right that anything with the ability to manifest the universe would be so insecure as to make requirements that remove spiritual free will, creating an inability for our souls to grow?

There is something within each of us that instinctively knows what is right, and not having access to this instinctive knowledge leads us to feeling hopeless, dissatisfied, unhappy or even unwell. It is my experience that interned ego disrupts this connection to our Creator and is the cause of the majority of our worldwide suffering.

Spiritual Healers

As I hope I have already shown, a spiritual healer is someone who has a profound relationship with the Absolute and is used as a vessel for the healing power of Spirit. In ancient Hebrew these people were referred to as Baal Shem, which means "master of the name," which implied that they led through the power of the divine name of God. In many cultures they are the humble medicine men, saints or psychics.

A spiritual healer must also be a medium/seer in all its forms, because all healing takes place in free will, and we have to have knowledge before we can have true free will. It is the seeing that paves the road to healing. Spiritual healers must be able to see and know before true healing can take place, or they might interrupt the free will of the client, that is, the free will of the individual's soul, not the free will of the body. The gift of sight combined with the energetic gift of healing allows for painless and natural removal of that which makes us ill. This preempts the long, arduous and harmful exorcisms performed today by well-intentioned people who do not have the gift of sight.

A healer is not someone who is trying to be important and considered special because of his gifts. The Baal Shem is a humble servant, with all the frailties of humanity.

Who are healers, and how do they get that way? Can anyone become a healer? Are true healers born and not made? Can the gifts of healing be developed over time? How many types of healers are there? How do we know if a healer is working in the light?

Do you see what I mean about there being a lot of unanswered questions? Let us first clarify the distinct difference between the healer and the gifts of healing. First and foremost, the healer is a human being with free will. The gifts of healing never compromise the free will of the healer. The healer has all of the same frailties as any human being and the same physical and emotional challenges. Healers are found throughout the world, many living ordinary lives, much like me.

Healers are individuals who choose to let Spirit use their existence to focus energy for the benefit of others. They are normal, everyday individuals who have decided, for various reasons, to use the gifts we can all access in some form or another. It is because I make this decision to be available that I can be used by the Absolute for healing as well as for the education of my soul.

We have been duped into thinking that healers are odd outcasts of society, when the fact is every person on the planet has gifts of healing (that darn language again). Isn't it interesting that so much effort has been directed toward eradicating something inborn and natural to all of us? It is primarily a lack of knowledge that has allowed this situation to persist. Ignorance and denial are the most seductive tools of greed and power.

A healer is somebody who develops a personal, experiential relationship with what we call the divine and uses his or her past as a tool kit from which to learn and grow. Healers do not always achieve a state in which they can be of full use to the Absolute, as that requires a great deal of psychological and spiritual work. It requires them, like all of us, to go beyond ego and deal with their fears.

In most cultures around the world, healers feel separated from mainstream society and can become isolated, causing them to stop using their gifts. Isolation prevents personal growth, inhibiting us from reaching the full potential of our giftedness. From a very early age, gifted people, particularly in Western societies, often have had feelings of isolation. There is rarely anyone, even within their family, who can help them with their "unusual" perception of the world. Because of this lack of context, the gifted grow up in a world that is cold and painful *to them*, especially considering the fact that we are all, by nature, social beings.

Gifted children are particularly sensitive and aware of the individual needs of all the people around them. They are naturally compassionate and empathetic, which means they feel the pain within those with whom they come in contact. They see, touch and feel their own pain, but they also see and feel the pain of others. They are keenly aware of their teacher's bad day, bad year and bad life, and of the other children's physical, emotional and psychological issues pertaining to their family lives, yet they have developed no context in which to put this information. The world can very easily crush the gifted young child. Western society examines these children and likes to categorize them as mentally ill, week minded etc. whereas many non-Western societies hold gifted people in high esteem.

Because of the lack of recognition for the gifts of every individual, those people recognized as gifted are usually overcome with requests. With their personal boundaries destroyed, they can become ill and even die. When a truly gifted healer's abilities become public knowledge, she is either shunned or flocked to, either of which makes her life very difficult. She may be raised to the status of a miracle worker or reduced to doing the devil's work. Either experience is damaging and false and causes the healer much strife and difficulty in this life. I have to be very careful in what I tell my children to say at school when they are asked about their father and what I do for a living. The last thing I want is for my children to be mistreated in any way because people misunderstand or fear what I do.

Some societies isolate the gifted to indoctrinate them into a certain belief system. A child that loses the opportunity for his or her brain to mature normally in this way can lose the understanding and compassion for other human beings that would otherwise develop. The gifted brain needs to develop as all others do, because the gift is not the brain; it is, in fact, what the individual is able to receive and reflect from Spirit. The brain is a finite biochemical mass that cannot even begin to hold the infinite knowledge of other human beings and the universe, as Spirit can. Consequently, it is imperative for the gifted to develop with other human beings of their own age in order to learn compassionate detachment. This detachment allows the healer to be of service without taking on the other person's issues. Conversely, compassionate *attachment*, or empathy, implies an agenda, not innocence. The agenda might be to please the client, or to achieve a miraculous healing, or to accomplish some other goal. It is detachment that allows for truly deep compassion with no bias.

Gifted individuals are able to access the fund of knowledge that existed before their present lifetime. This wisdom often causes them to be described from a very young age as "old souls." Access to this vast knowledge allows the healer to accept our physical manifestations as a part of the free will of the soul. This makes healers more useful to the Absolute, and it is this access to knowledge that is often referred to as the "gift of faith." The gift of knowing provides the healer with knowledge from the Absolute as to the purpose of life and death, allowing the individual with such a gift to approach a suffering or inquiring fellow human with compassionate detachment.

Because of their gifts and knowledge, healers are caught in a position of conflict: Their bodies are in the physical world and thus have all the needs of the body – food, warmth, clothes, shelter and other creature comforts – yet they have the possibility for so much more. They have to gain maturity and deal with the issues of genetics, siblings, trauma, narcissism, obsessions, ego and providing for themselves and their families, just like everyone else, while trying to find a clean path to Spirit. On top of this, they have to learn to see, feel, hear and navigate in the rest of the universe with Spirit, angels and guides while learning discernment and understanding predatory energy. As you can imagine, this would be a daunting task in a world that is neutral to their gifts and helps them explore their growing knowledge of Spirit. But, in a world that is bent on controlling the Absolute's ability to work with us individually, in a world that is greedy and hungry for power, in a world where many leaders are full of pride and ego, it is an uphill battle all the way. Healers who have been born with the gift of sight and have received the gift of faith have no interest in controlling the world. They are humble because they have a knowing that life in this physical world is a small, temporary aspect of our souls' progression.

With so much acting against them and a world unforgiving of their mistakes, healers, as prone to making mistakes as anyone else, sometimes hide from their issues or try to go it alone. Foolish pride can easily get in the way. Pride is an emotion that indicates ego; it leads an individual to hide from God's help. Because pride masks self-truth, a healer can begin to fool himself into thinking he can control his gift. The gift then becomes stagnant and disconnects from the system of social checks and balances, based on working together, as God intended. Once the ego is working alone, the healer feels vulnerable and can easily fall into the private hell of the "personal process." He might use his gifts as best he can, but will fall short of his or his clients' expectations. In turn, he will become frustrated and attempt to control his gifts more, falling into a never-ending cycle of self-doubt and destruction of those gifts, which negatively impacts clients and creates even more suspicion and hostility toward healers.

In the earliest recorded societies, medicine men, shamans and oracles were honored for their abilities. Pilgrims sought them out, often at great personal hardship, in order to seek healing of many sorts. These gifted people were relied upon for information about weather, crop planting, and the use of herbs and medicines, childbirth and all types of physical and mental illnesses. They were even used as the earliest X-ray devices, "seeing" illnesses and diseases that weren't visible on the surface. Because of these seemingly inexplicable abilities, those in power, such as tribal chiefs and elders, feared healers. Imagine how grateful ordinary people would be for these services, and how they would naturally look up to healers for their wisdom and assistance. It does not take much imagination to see how this natural gift would threaten those holding the reins of power, forced to deal with a gift that could not be controlled or bought.

Persecution of healers grew out of the desire to control the tribe. This is ironic, considering it was the healers who actually helped the tribe thrive. Tribal leaders who wanted status and honor exclusively for themselves resorted to rule by fear and intimidation as a way of exercising their authority. As we all know, while this may work in the short term, it creates a seedbed for discontent and rebellion. The natural, as opposed to contrived, authority of the gift of healing has always threatened those in power. It is this climate of fear that has caused healers to generate personal agendas in order to survive. Once a healer has an agenda, his gifts will stagnate and cease to grow. Healers can become corrupt, just like other human beings. They are, first and foremost, human and, as such, have free will. They may choose to align themselves with the prevailing leaders in order to survive, and thus put the purity of the gift in jeopardy.

Understanding What We Are Working With

Because the gifts of healing can be found in each of us, it is possible to have "less experienced souls" exhibit varying levels of these gifts. These people do not have the experience and knowing to fully develop and apply their gift, and so they can be easily persuaded to use their gifts for personal and institutional gain. Therefore, it is imperative that healers learn how to recognize, or discern, negative forces that might be influencing them. This is why a healer must pursue continuous spiritual growth as well as self-examination, in order to turn ego into a balancing tool , which is less corruptible. This way of life is directly linked to being used by the Absolute for deeper and more phenomenal types of healing.

I once treated a very tall, gifted healer who was proud of her ability to channel an angel and give people advice. Though she saw herself as successful publicly, her personal life was not so good. She wanted to have children but could not conceive, and her overall health was extremely poor. During her healing process I saw what she was doing, and my Guides instructed me to tell her to command the angel she had been channeling to show its true form. When she did this, she was immediately shown ten demons that revolted her so much she almost vomited. She realized that all her channeling of "angels" was really predatory energy with which she had been mistakenly working. She immediately stopped all her channeling work and soon afterwards became pregnant. Nine months later she gave birth to a healthy baby. Her physical body had become polluted by the dark energy she had been playing host to and, once she became aware of what she was really doing, she made a choice out of free will to banish the energy and stop the process. Her physical health was then able to return.

As you can see, even a gifted individual capable of working effectively within the energy of the Absolute can unknowingly work with energy that might cost him/her a great deal. In this case, the woman's health declined and she could not have a child because the energy she was working with interrupted her free will; "it" wanted her undivided attention. This cannot happen when working with Spirit. This story demonstrates the critical importance of learning how to discern what type of energy we are working with, as well as the powerful importance of the gift of command. Dark energy is susceptible to our command and must reveal its true 'colors' when commanded to do so.

The ability to become a healer is a result of soul progression, among other things. Soul progression is the spiritual growth needed to access the fund of knowledge that existed before this life. This gift is earned by an individual soul that has demonstrated a profound ability to understand the separate existence of the physical and the spiritual while residing within a physical body. In order to use the gift, one has to be a humble, willing soul, with the will to heal oneself. Healers must have a passion for healing and a willingness to surrender their egos when using their gifts. Many people with these gifts aren't effective because they're working in the wrong energy, are prideful and/or have their own agendas. In the case of the channeler above, she thought she was working in the light and helping people, but she also took pride in the fact that she could channel and give people advice, which in turn controlled their lives and compromised their free will. It was this attitude that allowed her to be working in predatory energy. Spirit never gives direct advice, which should be a litmus test for all healers using their gifts.

Another litmus test is the condition of the healer after performing a healing: is he or she drained emotionally or physically? You may have seen "psychics" collapse in exhaustion after a session. True healers who are allowing Spirit to work with them rather than trying to force their gifts should be no more tired than anyone else performing the same level of physical activity. If this is not the case, then the healer has been getting in the way or the "healing" has been taking the healer's personal energy. Either way, the necessary boundaries aren't being enforced, and this opens up the possibility that the healer is working in energy other than Spirit, such as human energy, collective energy or even predatory energy.

Human energy is used when one person consciously manipulates another person's energy. One example of this is the practice of Reike, which, as you will remember, is a therapy that produces the physical manipulation of molecular energy, which can then result in the movement of spiritual energy. For example, when someone puts his or her hands over you, you will often feel heat. That is the effect of two opposing charged energies coming into contact with each other. This often happens in massage and acupuncture as well.

Collective energy is the human energy of many people all focused at the same time on the same object with the same intention or desired outcome. Tent revivals are common sites for this type of experience, which occasionally results in a type of spiritual healing, though it is often temporary and is sometimes referred to as the placebo effect. The Absolute works in all ways, but this utilization of collective energy does not produce a consistent result because it does not provide any education of the soul.

I've been told that in today's New Age culture, exhibitions of collective energy are known as a "seminar high." There are apparently even "seminar groupies" who follow teachers and presenters on their lecture circuits and speak of the amazing feelings and "connections with the flow" they feel during these seminars. The "high" usually wears off after a few days.

Channeling is the practice of receiving messages, ideas or information from the spirit world through various methods. A medium is someone who is able to convey messages to living people from the spirits of the dead. The difference between mediums and channelers is that mediums simply pass on messages, whereas a specific energy or entity can take over the channeler's body, mind and soul and, in effect, inhabit that person's body. The channeler often speaks and moves quite differently when inhabited. Whenever I have asked channelers where they go during their channeling sessions, they typically respond with, "I don't know" or "I just leave my body." You begin to see my concern. Because the body-soul union is the sacred gift of life from the Absolute, nothing from Spirit would ever interrupt it. The Absolute does not need to be channeled or in any way interrupt the body-soul union.

I feel mediums that become drained or are nagged by spirits from the other side are also allowing themselves to be used improperly. These spirits are attacking their free will and boundaries because the mediums do not fully understand how to use the protection and boundary process of Spirit. This protection does not allow the individual to be violated in any way. The body-soul union, the gift of life from the Absolute, should never be compromised during spiritual work. It has been my experience that, if it is compromised, something isn't right, and the gifted individual requires more learning.

You will remember the incident from the early days of my practice when I was working on a client with Bob and I took on an angry predatory energy from the client's heart chakra. This energy sensed a weakness in my etheric system similar to that of the client and which I had not yet processed. The next thing I knew, I felt something clutching my heart, trying to stop it from beating. Fortunately, with the help of Bob and my Guides, I recovered from what could have been a catastrophic incident. This event was designed to teach me several things. As Christ told us, no one doing the work of the divine will ever be physically harmed. I thought I was dying, and I had to learn to trust in the Absolute, even in the most life threatening of crises. It taught me the importance of having clear energetic boundaries in place before working on a client, and the importance of continually questioning myself and doing my own education of the soul. It also taught me to be ever humble and always ask for the proper protection from each client's energy.

Mediums possess wonderful gifts which should be grown and developed into full spiritual healing gifts. It is incumbent and imperative for us to continually examine ourselves, our motives and issues and do our own psychological work as we grow our gifts. If, however, the medium continues to spend her time in this one facet of her gifts, i.e. speaking to the dead, and becomes drained or compromised in any way, then she needs to question and explore what is draining her. It is a common myth that spiritual healers must be exhausted in order to demonstrate their prowess or success. It is this physical exhaustion that can force them into becoming trapped at a dead end where their gifts are used up, in a sense, without further development.

We all have the capability to connect with the spirit world. The question we need to be mindful of is, "Why do we want to?" Are you doing this to become rich and famous, to have power over other people or to honor and develop your soul? I do not want to discourage gifted channelers and mediums, but rather encourage them to further develop their gifts and become full-fledged spiritual healers. True channelers and mediums are gifted people who need the benefit of the checks and balances of working together with other spiritual healers. Every medium and channeler can function as a spiritual healer if they continue to develop and grow in their spirituality and do their personal work of the soul. We are here to help each other do just that.

Every time I work on an individual it is a different experience. If I come to a session with preconceived ideas, I am limiting Spirit as to how it should be working. If I think a session must be a struggle of faith between good and evil, then that is where the session will stagnate. It is my job to be clear of ego and allow Spirit to do what is needed. I cannot know what is needed. I must have a clear willingness to allow Spirit to work with me, nothing more and nothing less. I think it is this simple and straightforward nature of spiritual healing that makes it so wonderful and also so threatening to others, especially those who feel the need to define and control Spirit within specific constructs. Spirit, as far as I experience it, does not have an allegiance to any particular belief system. It has an allegiance only to humanity. It is the experience of the Absolute's love for us all.

One of the first things I learned about being a spiritual healer is that I don't own this gift. It can be shut down at any time, because it does not come from me. It comes from the Absolute. This gift evolves, and it requires me to evolve and mature in innocence and without ego in the negative sense. I am merely a tool through which Spirit can focus energy for the human experience of learning. If ever I think I must use a certain technique, I am limiting Spirit. Therefore, I always ask my Guides questions to ensure that I am a clear vessel for Spirit. I must be careful not to cling to ritual or expectations, but be forever open to the wonder and the unknowable possibilities of the Absolute. Spirit can use anyone at any given time for the healing of another. I am one of those people who were born with a fairly evolved gift of healing which may be looked at as a more advanced "tool." As I continue to work on clients, my knowledge and, therefore, a skill of sort, has evolved. I have developed greater understanding and knowing of the things Spirit asks me to do. However, I do not personally employ any of this knowledge when working on another; I remain in wonderment and innocence as Spirit does its work.

There are valuable techniques taught throughout the world that can inspire one to become a better "tool." However, when people become invested in the techniques, they effectively limit themselves and remove themselves from the limitless possibilities of Spirit. I am not saying it isn't important to work on improving techniques. What I am saying is the most important techniques are innocence and a direct relationship with Spirit. There is no place for ego in spiritual healing.

My Gift of Faith

One particularly grey winter day, in my nineteenth year, I decided to visit my mother. I'd been feeling rather depressed and thought a short trip out of town might be better than hanging around my apartment, feeling sorry for myself. I packed a few things and took off for the small island where she lived.

I arrived midmorning on a Saturday and spent some time talking with my mom about my life, the pressures of college, and the unsettling emptiness I was feeling. I just couldn't seem to make any sense of my life right then, or of the melancholy feeling that seemed to have a hold over me. Mom, true to form, had learned about a party going on that night. She seemed always to know what was going on around the island. She knew the young woman hosting the party and promptly introduced us and, at that point, I was led away to a gathering of people I didn't know because "it would do me some good."

The party consisted of a group of people from a local church, very clean-cut and not at all what I was used to. There was no drinking and I couldn't even say the "F" word without fear of getting tossed out on my ear. The party was even chaperoned! I started casing the room for a quick, easy exit; then I remembered I had no car. I felt trapped, without wheels at a party of strangers.

I began to realize I was with a group of people who had very few life experiences. They were extremely innocent regarding the ways of the world because they had been raised in a protected, somewhat idyllic, Christian fundamentalist environment. They didn't understand me and I didn't understand them.

They began to talk about their Christian beliefs, and I began to panic as I realized they were "born again," and here I was, a Catholic, and not much of one, at that. When they asked me about my religious beliefs, I rolled my eyes up in my head and thought, "Oh, no!" I thought, if I can't dazzle them with my brilliance, I'll baffle them with my bull. The conversation went on into the night, debating Catholicism and born-again Christianity. It was actually good for me because it was the first time I had discussed my personal beliefs with peers. I ended up promising to go to church with them the following weekend.

Then I met Matt, with whom I seemed to have more in common, due in part to our shared experiences as the children of narcissistic fathers. Matt's father wasn't as violent as mine, but he had left when Matt was six, just as my father had done. We soon began sharing stories of our past and realized we harbored similar anger and resentment toward our fathers. Out of our rocky beginning, an alliance grew.

I would occasionally drive to the island to visit my mom and would meet up with Matt. We even attended his church together on a few of my visits. It was on one of those occasions that I received what I would later call my "Gift of Faith." One particular Sunday morning my friend and I arrived early at church to get a good seat. Only a few people had arrived, so we went to the front pew. We both sat down and leaned forward to put our knees on the kneeler. I laid my head in my hands to say a little prayer, and suddenly I was somewhere else. I mean I was literally, completely unaware of my body, and I was walking with what I thought was Jesus. There was no sensation of movement or sense of contact with my body. I was told many things which have subsequently unfolded, as stated, as my life has progressed. The walk and talk with Jesus seemed to last forever, and yet it was as if no time had passed. Just as suddenly, I was back in the church pew as before, waiting for the service to begin. Matt was at my side, firmly elbowing me. I told him to stop, as people arriving for the service would not appreciate such activity up in the front row. He looked at me, dumbstruck: Not only had the congregation arrived and found seats, but the service had been started and concluded; we were the only ones left in church. He said he had been elbowing me for an hour and a half!

I separate this experience from the knowledge and act of religious faith, as they are very different experiences. This is not the "belief in an institution or a strongly held set of beliefs without logical proof" as defined by Webster's dictionary. It is the experience of the loving embrace of the Absolute, as described by the mystics of all religions. This difference is an important element of spiritual healing because it is a validation beyond all words and logic. Faith is, first and foremost, an experience of the divine. It is a knowing beyond the physical understanding of the world that comes from a direct experience of the Absolute.

Evil, the Introject, and Why Bad Things Happen to Good People

I am constantly asked, "Did God create evil? If so, why?" As with everything else, what is described as "evil" was, indeed, created by the Absolute, but not for the purpose of causing harm to us or anyone else.

It was developed as a perfect learning tool to promote the evolution of the species.

It is our body's nature to conserve energy. When our immediate physical needs are met, we become fat and happy, so to speak. To get us out of our comfort zone, we need a push, and that push is the "Introject." The Introject is most commonly defined in psychological terms as the inner, negative, parental voice taken on by a child that reinforces fear-based beliefs, including the threat to withhold love if the individual does not conform. As a psychological term, used in its basic meaning, introject is an attitude or idea that has been unconsciously incorporated into one's personality. In Eternal Psychology™ the Introject has been imbued with elemental energy and feeds off the fear energy of the host to maintain its existence. Think of it as an energy vampire that eventually creates enough internal discomfort to force us to search for happiness; we have been wired to internally create the grist that has moved us beyond the cave. This inner voice preys on a person's sense of safety and ability to be loved. Today's common psychological definition identifies it as the assuming of a negative message. I'm taking it one step further when I describe it as a self-generated, energetic, internal defense elemental. A child develops this internal elemental to keep itself safe in the early years of life.

The Absolute created an energy force and gave it the job of creating the grist, or the Introject, necessary to encourage human beings to move out of caves into modern civilization, to change, in effect, from a less perfect vessel of learning to today's more evolved learning vessel. This energy force has been called "evil," "Lucifer," "the devil" and many other names, but all conjure up too many distracting images

169

in today's society, so for the sake of discussion, I am going to use a term given to me by my Guides – the Raptive. Having been given the job, however, the Raptive took the ball and ran with it a little too far. In fact, instead of simply administering the Introject, the Raptive identified so closely with it that it actually evolved to become that force.

The term "rapt" means "involved in, fascinated by or concentrating on something to the exclusion of everything else," or "showing or suggesting deep emotions of joy or ecstasy." So perhaps a concise definition of the Raptive would be "that which is enthralled and captivated by itself." It became deeply satisfied with itself and felt ecstatic at what it was created to do, to the extent that it felt it no longer needed a connection to the Absolute and, in fact, now attempts to interrupt and take control of our connection to the Absolute which is within all of us. This energy is a pervasive persuader and is often successful at seducing us away from our own inner connection with the Absolute. Humans are easily distracted, as when we're hungry and can think of nothing else but food. Our minds also tend to drift toward 'forbidden' thoughts. If you tell yourself not to think about something, chances are your mind will often go back to that very thing. That is what makes the Raptive so effective.

One very important fact to remember, however, is that the Introject, when created, was made subject to our spiritual free will. That is why the Raptive, or evil, is completely at our command. It will try to control us, deceive us and trick us in every way in order to stay in control. Its goal is to separate us from the Absolute and, therefore, to stop our evolution as a species. It wants to control our connection to the

Absolute. It can puff itself up, take on the form of our worst fears or hide in the form of our desires, but, at the end of the day, we will still always have command over it. We simply need to know this and use our power.

Because the Introject is designed to help us learn, it is always subject to free will. If you are given incorrect change in your favor, you have the opportunity for a learning moment. You will exercise your free will and either learn that the truth will set you free, or you can lie by omission, make a buck and learn from your guilt. It is the challenges of our existence that help us learn and grow. No pain, no gain. Evil was designed to give us grist for our learning mill, and that is all it can do.

The thing we call evil comes in many forms, but, in the end, it is all subject to the control we each give it. This forces it to hide in language and fear in order to create the illusion of power. As M. Scott Peck stated in his book *People of the Lie* (Touchstone, 1998), "Evil, once identified, is easily commanded."

The most important fact to know about evil is this: it is not intrinsically powerful. It has only the power we give it. We grant it power through "human evil," which is used by the Raptive to create false fear and confusion. I always see it portrayed puffed up like a paper dragon from one of those Chinese New Year parades. This type of energy particularly tries to scare all seers, especially when young, to establish a precedent in their minds, as it is the adult seers that might easily identify and rid us all of this energy. If it can scare the seer, then it can continue to use both the seer and the host human. Our cultural difficulties in defining, describing and agreeing upon what evil actually is serve as prime examples of human evil. Many of us don't believe in evil, due, in part, to the way it is portrayed. If we can't agree on it, or don't believe it exists, then it has free rein to work without interference.

In doing my own homework for the soul, I learned about this Introject concept and was subsequently shown it in my clients. I was now able to see this specific energy in my clients when it was presented for their learning process, and I came to the conclusion that the Introject is the most intimate of our elementals, affecting our thought processes. We develop it in early childhood when we feel afraid and unsafe. It resonates with our deepest fears and longings, and, therefore, has the strongest hold on us, energetically speaking, of anything I have seen in my work with people.

Perversely, we develop a fondness for and familiarity with that which causes us pain, or grist, much like hostage victims who form attachments to their captors, described as the "Stockholm Syndrome" after a famous incident in 1973 in which several hostage victims of a bank robbery resisted rescue attempts and refused to testify against their captors. We become obsessed with making the abusers understand us. We want them to know just how much they are hurting us. This desire gives them power in our psyches. When we give power to an elemental, or thought, it keeps us from being grounded in our own adult truth. We stay stuck in confusion, doubt and victim-energy, all of which interrupt our experience of the Absolute.

As with any protective device, when we no longer need it, or we outgrow it, it holds us back and can cause severe damage. Imagine having to sit in your infant car seat at age thirty. Ouch! The Introject has a vested interest in keeping us unreasonably fearful and self-limiting. Once discovered and fully understood, it will simply have to go.

When my clients are ready to understand this energy and have it removed, it is only because they have done their psychological homework. Once the energy is removed, clients will often need more assistance with curtailing the lifelong habits and thoughts generated by their Introjects. I can personally say that this can be very difficult but rewarding psychological work, and it is a necessary part of the process of developing one's gifts as a spiritual healer.

Because this Introject elemental was developed within us, it does not have an energy source of its own. It needs to "feed" energetically, which it does by keeping us in fear and doubt. It hides in our deepest thoughts and continues to whisper to us reasons to be afraid and stuck in our current stage of development. This fear makes our energy systems weak, puts our chakras out of alignment and leads to physical illness and injury, and these trends will continue until the Introject is removed. It can be removed only in a healing session with full knowledge of what it did for us, and, therefore, with gratitude for how it kept us safe when we were young. I believe, and my collaborating therapists and my clients believe, that this is one of the most important areas where psychotherapy and spiritual healing can work together to provide more effective and deeper healing.

An effective psychotherapist, using techniques such as EMDR and Lifespan Integration, can effectively remove the physical energy of a trauma or troubling incident. The spiritual energy, however, needs to be removed by a healer who can see. When I do this for a client who has been working with a therapist at this level, the learning process and, therefore, the release of this energy goes very quickly. I am directed to work with the client to find out why he or she initially manifested the thought processes, for what learning purpose. Once this is understood, the removal of the Introject habit is possible.

As I mentioned earlier, the physical body has a will of its own, and part of this imperative is the will to survive, protect your clan and, therefore, dominate. As populations grew, we created civilizations, and that forced the issue of crowd control. Laws, trends of behavior, belief systems, and cultural codes (manners) allowed clans to coexist. Human evil is the reaction society has to those who act against or outside of the prevailing culture. Human evil is actually much harder to control than spiritual evil. This is why the Raptive preys on human evil, in order to hide within it and, therefore, maintain its existence and delusions of power. Human evil is the act of preying upon one another for reasons that do not matter to the Absolute, the minutiae of daily life. Spiritual evil is energy preying upon those things that *do* matter to the Absolute, such as the interruption of free will and anything that disrupts the body-soul union.

Having said that, evil is not weak. It has all the power of all the human elementals. I have been picked up and thrown across the room by evil in the early days of my practice. I have been deceived and manipulated by it, which is why I always remember to command whatever energy I see, even my Guides, the Holy Spirit and Christ energy, to show its true colors.

Evil is feared, but it cannot create fear. It must prey on ours, such as the fear of the unknown and past injustices, in order to create bigotry and disharmony. It cannot create hatred. It uses our ignorance and our pack mentality to isolate or bind us. It cannot directly control us unless we are ignorant or confused as to its true nature. It uses our own apathy, denial and confusion to manipulate and control us and breed more ignorance and divisiveness. It uses our past fears and hurts to stagnate us and keep us from the Absolute; thus we cease to evolve spiritually and remain a playground for its existence.

In order to combat evil, someone has to blow the whistle and say, "stop." That is one of my many messages for this book. Let's drag this thing out into the light of day and know it for what it is. We no longer need to live in fear of evil. We can shine the light of awareness and truth on it. We must allow knowledge of evil and common purpose to inform us as a culture and a species. It's time for a paradigm shift. We need to allow for the differences between cultures, religions and political systems. We need to allow for the growth of our species and acknowledge the purpose of our sacred body-soul union, which is the education of the soul. Until we acknowledge the sacredness of all human beings, we will stagnate in ignorance, divisiveness, jealousies and war, all products of evil's influence.

Chapter Eight: Developing and Working with Discernment

One of my objectives in writing this book is to bring to light the sad fact that we are not using the gifts of the divine to anywhere near the potential intended. These gifts are designed to enhance the entire human experience within the bounds of spiritual free will, educating the soul for the progression of the divine. I also want to encourage dialogue and further understanding of these gifts and the ways in which they can be used in service to humankind. It is my belief, not that we all need to become spiritual healers/mediums, but rather that we all should engage in educating ourselves and continuing our spiritual growth. I have been shown that a world of divergent cultures has created fear that has effectively locked this birthright away.

We have heard for years that "we" are on the threshold of a worldwide paradigm shift. That this paradigm shift is a "shift" toward working in "the light," so we can be of service to all humankind. It all sounds great, but the concept is extremely unfocused and left open to misinterpretation by the naive and the unscrupulous. We all try to help each other and be of service in some way; it's natural, and our religions are role models and maps to this behavior. However, we have not developed a common, innocent platform on which to build this shift. I am shown this platform as the ability to bring the divine into our daily lives. This is our birthright, and yet this construct eludes us. I have been shown that if we rethink our perspective on evil, (using evil for growth, as intended, instead of letting ourselves be used by "it" through fear), we will move in the right direction. Further, if we rethink our position on spiritual gifts, global community and our souls' progression, we will all make this "paradigm" shift. We can then educate ourselves as a species, out of the chaos and into our eternal birthright.

Discerning is the most important gift to be understood when working with all the spiritual gifts. Our ability to discern the Absolute has been sorely confused by so many well-meaning (and not-so-well-meaning) individuals, that we have nearly lost this ability altogether. As a result, we've lost our trust in our own ability to connect with and accurately discern the Absolute. I see it every day in my practice, and it is echoed in the practices of my colleagues. I have been shown over and over that our ability to connect with the Absolute is straightforward, clear and free of prejudice. It does not conform to any dogma or other requirements created by humans. The Absolute has no agenda as to when we learn and progress spiritually. The timetable is all left to the individual's free will.

If we understand that our souls exist forever and that this life is a step in the education of our soul, discernment begins to take on new meaning. Discernment becomes the key to spiritual progression and everything that effort entails. It does not manifest with any sense of urgency. It is a naturally occurring knowing that we all have. If it feels urgent, it is not of the divine; it is ego-based. We cannot get rid of ego. It can be used as a tool either to free us into soul progression or to force us to submit to our own fears and the grist that free will requires.

When I am taught something in my life, sometimes I become angry if the lesson comes in an uncomfortable way. I react in ego, like everyone does. But there is always a gem of sincere learning as I struggle with the lesson I've manifested. A perfect example of this occurred when I experienced painful kidney stones that prevented me from seeing clients as a spiritual healer. Although physical pain is not my preferred method of learning, it did get the message across that I needed to concentrate on writing this book instead of seeing clients. Many people became angry with me for my decision, adding social discomfort to the physical pain.

I used to wonder at the irony of why I, of all people, would be called upon to write this book. After all, you would think someone with dyslexia would not be the best man for the job. However, I now think there are a few "learning gems" in this as well. My difficulties with reading and writing have led me to seek help from, and work more closely with, many wonderful people, which, in turn, expanded our mutual practices and knowledge bases. As a result we are able to offer more complete healing to our clients than we could have offered separately. The "gift of dyslexia" makes it difficult for me to read quickly. Therefore, I remain somewhat limited in my access to published information, which requires me to stay connected to my Guides for my source of information. That procedure ensures this book expresses a direct link to Spirit rather than filtering the message through what I might have read. I'm not saying reading is bad, (I do read well, just more slowly than average) but I feel that, in allowing the information to come through me directly from my Guides, I can pass it on to you without any preconceived or ego-driven agenda. I have learned about my gifts experientially. I find comfort in reading that others have experienced the same or similar lessons. This also demonstrates that you can experience the Absolute in your own way, outside the box, if you will. In my case, dyslexia kept my relationship to my Guides experiential and innocent of academic influence as it was forming. I think this was the Absolute's way of helping me maintain innocence and proving to me that innocence is critical when discerning the Absolute.

It is true that, within each major religious construct, we are told not to "judge" others. It is this judgment that actually keeps humanity away from innocent discernment of the divine. When we judge others' experience of the divine, we are acting as a God. If we combine the aforementioned and the purpose of physical life, "to educate the soul," we can see that judgment keeps us from our main objective. It is like going to a university and studying mathematics only. When all is said and done, you come out with a Ph.D. in math, and you stand there at the podium, proclaiming that it's incomprehensible that anyone could have a Ph.D. in criminal law or art history, since you have not experienced that. How foolish!

Yet we are allowed by Spirit to believe in the path that brought each of us closer to the Divine. We are allowed to talk about this path with those who want to listen, as this might in fact help someone discover their path. But we are not allowed to judge another person or culture's path. To do so is to judge the Divine's omnipotence. This is the universal message given by Jesus, Mohammed and Siddhartha when they walked our planet. This is what every major spiritual teacher has tried to demonstrate with his or her life. Are the universality and consistency not amazing?

The one common element in the approach to the divine is innocence, or lack of ego. Some refer to this as "surrender," which can be a bit misleading if it is equated with giving up. (Some have reached their gifts by giving up their gift of humanity, but this is not practical for most, and it would have dire consequences for the human race if we all found our gifts this way!) In the appropriate type of surrender, we give up only our uneducated ego, and what we gain is the unconditional, never-ending love of the divine. We gain a personal connection with divine guidance.

The Ethics of Healing- Discernment

I have written about ethics throughout this book, but it is such an important aspect of spiritual healing that I want to touch on it again here. It is my experience with healers of all types that ethics are typically overlooked, ignored or flat-out bashed. Ethics have not been standardized, and yet they are the most important part of discernment.

I have been taught over and over again that I must always ask for permission to look into someone's energy. (We all pick up on indiscriminate elemental energy. This is why we are cautioned to be mindful of the energy of thought.) Without asking permission, I would be compromising that person's free will, which is totally unacceptable for any spiritual healer. Just because someone's ego wants to know something, that doesn't mean we have the right to seek that information. Just because we *can* see, that doesn't mean we *should*. It may make us more interesting and powerful to other people because we can "see and know" things that the average person cannot. However, it is wrong to do so without an individual's consent. It is my experience that doing so only shows the seer irrelevant, common or misconstrued information, because only elemental energy (again, the energy of life such as what we all experience in a busy city as compared to a walk through the forest) can be perceived from this perspective, and such energy is irrelevant except to preserve the somas. Yes the medium as well as every individual might be perceiving anger, frustration, human interaction of any sort, and it can be as clear as day to him or her. The problem is that this energy is the energy generated from thought; hence it can be random, fantasy, or emotion-driven. This information cannot be depended on for healing or education as we all have indiscriminate thought unattached to our beliefs or actions.

When a healer works directly with the individual, elemental energy has to be understood and moved to get "the rest of the picture." Elemental energy is a natural form of protection against energetic violation of personal privacy and guards against interruption of free will. Elementals contain a bit of emotional truth and, therefore, are easily misconstrued by all of us. It is the energy we all acknowledge when we sense that someone is having a bad day or is frustrated with something. We all use this energy to show compassion and empathy through common courtesy. We can use it to know when to be tender with someone or when to laugh and play with them.

Elemental energy is just enough truth to allow the medium to be caught in the snare of ego if they can't differentiate between this and what is sacred. Without permission, this is the only thing the medium can pick up on, and he will mistake it for that which is sacred. If the medium/ spiritual healer uses elemental energy as the truth to disarm or harm, then he is misusing the energy. It is this that compromises the gifts of the person performing the infringement and causes him to stagnate in his own ego. This ensures his gifts will not evolve. It also gives spiritual healing a bad name, and understandably so. If the medium acknowledges this energy only as any other human does, then it is relatively unimportant, sidelined, and utilized only to show compassionate love.

Can you imagine a dentist reaching into your mouth at a party without permission simply because he knows how? Or he suspects a cavity? Or a proctologist, for that matter? How rude! And yet, so many gifted people think nothing of looking into someone's sacred energy out of curiosity, ego or pride. (Remember, though, that they are mistaken to believe they can see anything more than elemental energy.) They might enjoy the notoriety and attention they get for this special ability. This is a purely ego-driven act that is not of service to anything but the medium's ego

Another relatively common unethical occurrence in this field is the telling of a specific individual's future. This predestines people's lives and, therefore, interrupts their free will. It is completely subject to our personal symbology and human frailties. Prophecy, as it is called, should be done only in groups of seven or more in order to counter our humanity. Seven is the appropriate number given in the bible, but it is also the number that has arisen in my own practice, the number required to counter the strong ego states that can be generated by the dramatic visions often shown during prophesying. If Nostradamos had not worked alone, might his visions have been more time sensitive, possibly less vague? Other seers, had they been present, might have asked the questions needed to explain the visions. Individuals accustomed to seeing such things would not be alarmed and, gathered together, they could ask good, intelligent questions pertinent to the visions. In meditation, each could have set the intention for the upcoming session. The result would be subtle variations in the message, opening a valuable dialogue more likely to lead to valid interpretations.

Now let's talk for a minute about channeling. As I've mentioned previously, nothing from Spirit even remotely suggests you turn over your body to an entity. That interrupts free will. Why would the Absolute grace each of us with the gift of the body-soul union, which we call life, and then interrupt it for the sake of a message of emotion? Communication with the Absolute can be effectively accomplished through the parameters of our energetic system. This is what the sixth and seventh chakras are intended for, among other things. We never need be compromised in order to communicate with the Absolute. Spirit will never compromise a gift you've already been given, such as the gift of life.

I once met a very gifted medium who had worked as a successful artist. She did not know she was a medium, so she went through a third of her adult life just accepting things she knew about other people. She had been taught as a child that this "stuff" was unsafe "voodoo." When she was in her thirties, she frequently had dreams of a certain being wishing to be involved with her life. The dreams were always pleasant enough, but it unsettled her when the dreams led to this personality trying to massage her ego into letting her become very "powerful" if it could just be within her body. Over the years the personality courted her into eventually just trying to let itself into her body so that she could feel powerful. During one particular down time in her life, when she was feeling powerless, the possibility of power became very tantalizing.

The entity or personality was able to merge with her. It felt all right, and she allowed it to happen again and again. Eventually she told a friend, who was naively impressed, causing the medium to feel even more powerful. Eventually this led to the woman actually giving readings to others. The information she provided was true, and soon people paid a great deal of money to see her. She felt even more powerful. The only catch was that, afterwards, she remembered nothing of the sessions. In fact, she did not even know what happened to her memory or where she went during these sessions. Eventually, as a demonstration of power, the woman was required by this personality to do personally violating rituals before each session so that her body would be clear for it to reside in. This would allow the sessions to get even better, she was promised. She succumbed to the rituals and the rave reviews increased.

The personality eventually said it wanted to share this experience with her clients to let them also enjoy this feeling of power. She advertised, and they came. The personality brought its friends in to let them enter the clients. The clients suddenly knew things about people, and they felt powerful. None of them knew what was happening to their bodies. None of them knew that they were being used for the entertainment of non-angelic energies. They did not realize that they were being used as the home for predatory energy.

This entire episode in the lives of these gifted people could have been avoided if only this uneducated "channeler" had found a place to go to ask questions and learn about her gifts. She could have been a great medium and possibly a healer if she had not been caught up in the courtship of a very seductive energetic personality. If the truth about predatory energy were available for all, instead of having it hidden away in the name of "God," she and many others would not become pawns for predatory energy.

Mediums, on the other hand, are a different story. Mediums are often confused with channelers, but true mediums are not violated. They remain present in their bodies while receiving information, knowing, pictures, or even words through the brain. It is paramount for such gifted people to maintain very clear boundaries; otherwise they can end up exhausted and haunted. As with all spiritually gifted individuals, mediums must constantly ask themselves for what purpose are they using their gifts. Is it to entertain friends at a party? To help one client at the expense of another? Are his or her efforts helping anybody? My Guides are explicit with me that these gifts are to be used only for healing and educating the soul, and only when requested.

Unfortunately, I have had contact with many gifted people who do not understand this rule. One such man, whom I'll call Al, is a successful medium who regularly looks into others people's energy fields at the request of his clients. He does not, however, have the permission of the person whose energy he is attempting to look into, and is, therefore, compromising it. In one instance, a friend told me that Al looked into the energy of several coworkers on behalf of a client who was going to have a high-pressure meeting with them and was feeling nervous and insecure. In his own mind, the client wanted to walk into the meeting feeling self-assured. He asked Al about these three individuals, and Al looked into them. In one woman's energy he saw what he interpreted as breast cancer. The medium had no idea about the history of the woman and did not have an understanding of elemental or physical energy. The news naturally upset his client, who then felt the need to tell his coworker about her cancer.

This information was most distressing to the woman because it came from a well-known medium through a "friend and colleague." What Al did, in effect, was create a powerful negative elemental that set this woman up for manifesting cancer. As it turned out, the lady did not have cancer, but her neighbor had breast cancer, creating the elemental thought energy that was perceived as cancer from the perspective of the unscrupulous medium. A demonstration of incomplete elemental energy!

Mediums must also be able to discern whether the information they are receiving feeds the ego of the entity supplying it and is not in the best interests of the client. I have witnessed entities barge in to a healing session, so to speak, and demand to be heard. I have been taught this is highly suspect and is an indication the entity is trying to avoid its own learning process. My guidance has been to always require the entity to come in through Spirit. This ensures that it is there for the benefit of the client. If it refuses to do so, then it obviously has a personal agenda, usually about avoiding its own learning process, and I banish it from the session.

Ethics require and support spiritual responsibility. Ethics develop naturally as you are able to realign ego, as you recognize and fully comprehend the body-soul union and its purpose. Compassionate detachment follows this understanding, and, with compassionate detachment, one is able to develop faith in the Absolute and what binds us to the omnipotent. This, in turn, sustains us in our innocent understanding of what is truly a priority for the client beyond anything we may personally think. This is how all gifted people can work and be of service without endangering the free will of the client or others. It is a code of ethics that provides a natural system of checks and balances with people who have connected with their energetic gifts. If the ego is present, it influences when and how people use their gifts, and then the gifts will stop awakening. This creates a natural glass ceiling beyond which the gifts will not progress unless and until the healer continues in his or her own personal education of the soul.

Chapter Nine: Educating the Soul—What's Next

A client was referred to me from a therapist. As usual, the therapist did not give me much information about this person. She told me she felt the client could benefit from some time spent in a healing session. She gave the man my phone number, but he did not call. The therapist told me she had suggested several times over a period of a year that the person might call me. He had not called; in fact, the client did not go to therapy sessions regularly and, when he did show up, the progression was like pulling taffy.

At some point he called me and wanted an appointment. I informed him I needed to meditate with his Guides before our session, to be shown the basics for the session. The client agreed. His Guides were very direct with me. During the meditation they showed me he had PTSD (post traumatic stress disorder). The client didn't understand it or think it was true. I told him that I was not a therapist, so I could not diagnose; I just pass the information on.

During the healing session, his Guides began to show me pictures of events in his past. He immediately recognized these events and was quite suddenly able to fully engage his memories. Apparently some of these were events he had talked about in therapy, but he hadn't been able to engage with the trauma of them. He saw them more as unfortunate or anecdotal stories from his past. As the session progressed, he connected emotional and energetic aspects of the events. He indicated to me that a door was opening to the truth within his experience of these events. He felt many sensations within his body as the trauma began to surface.

I saw him again at a date of his choosing. When we sat down for the second session, he opened up to more events beyond those of the previous session. He indicated that session had in fact made available to him memories long forgotten. He recalled many more memories that I had not seen, and he mentioned that, during his sessions with his therapist, they had indeed discussed his PTSD, but he had been unable to connect anything to it until now. He said now it all made perfect sense to him. We moved through this session, and I was shown some physical ailments that were manifested now that his memory block had been lifted. This type of breakthrough is typical of the experiences I have in my healing sessions.

The man later told me these two sessions had allowed him to complete a great deal of psychological processing and healing he had been searching for his entire adult life. This interim seemed to open up many more subsequent avenues for psychological processing that could not have been opened previously. He also indicated, at last check, his physical ailments were reduced greatly.

Spiritual healing and psychotherapy work well together, as the story above demonstrates. In all healing modalities, when an individual doesn't seem able to incorporate the therapy, a session of spiritual healing and, *possibly*, a follow-up with a psychotherapist, can identify and remove the energetic blocks, clearing the way for the benefits of the physical therapies and Psychotherapy.

Conscious understanding (generating free will) by the client is usually necessary in order for us to work with their "issues" on an energetic level. Through free will by education, trauma and opportunistic energy can be released easily, with authority. With new realizations and removal of the energy of events the client can easily move forward in his psychological processing. Spiritual healing can remove the blocking energy that still exists after events. Healing can virtually un-stick clients so psychotherapists can employ the tools they have been taught to create new healthy synapses.

Spiritual healing is necessary for removal of the Introject as well. Remember, the Introject is unseen and becomes an irritant. The client has to have "done the homework" in the psychotherapy sessions or on their own, by learning to recognize the attributes of the Introject. The client must learned why he or she developed this outdated defense mechanism in the first place. Once this is accomplished the internal elemental energy can be removed making room for positive energy.

The processing and understanding have to come full circle, or we will continue to manifest the same circumstances in order to educate the soul. If energy is removed before the root understanding then the work is almost pointless. We cannot bypass our learning curves, as this would be removing the purpose of life, to learn what it is to be human.

Once again, it is the collaboration of spiritual healing with psychotherapy which provides a much more complete and multidimensional healing for the client. My Guides, during a meditation session, have given me the term Eternal Psychology™ to identify this multidimensional approach to healing. It makes sense to me because this type of healing is for the soul, which is eternal. Physical healing benefits the body, which at some point will cease to exist, but our soul lives forever. Our physical body's only purpose is to be the vehicle for educating our soul; hence, all things that happen to us, including physical healing, also occur within this directive. Talk about getting more bang for your buck. The clients who do their personal work this way always seem to receive a deeper healing both psychologically and physically. The physical healings then become permanent. This is a timeless healing process which moves the soul along its journey to the Absolute.

Some time before the words were given to me, I noticed my practice moving into sync with several psychotherapy practices as we began to work with mutual clientele. The dynamic of Eternal Psychology™ developed naturally out of our clients' needs. We were working at this level long before we had a name for it. As with all aspects of this journey, with permission from the client, we would sometimes find it necessary and helpful to discuss the energetic and psychological aspects of a spiritual healing session with their therapist. Having information about the spiritual and energetic issues can provide the psychotherapist a deeper method of addressing the emotional issues confronting the client.

I have learned that our Guides know the keys to unlocking our journey to physical and mental health. Our clients do not necessarily agree with this process. The clients often think they know what is best. What I point out to them is that the process they own and identify with has not worked thus far, so why not try some new approach? Some clients simply cannot let go of preconceived notions of healing. Those who are able to drop their defenses and identifications with their injuries and let their Guides help, do get what they need. It was in this way our practices began to merge. We all see clients individually, although many of our clients prefer to work with this new, collaborative approach.

This has been quite a journey for me, and I imagine it will continue to unfold for all my years to come. Sometimes I look back over my life, my childhood, my coming-of-age years, and my time building a family and a business, and I am amazed at how things have turned out. Here I am, a very conventional guy, earning a living as a spiritual healer. How far from conventional have I gone? Or am I conventional now?

I must say, I have days when I really wonder how this all happened. Not the actual events, because I'm fully aware of those. What I wonder about is just who I am and how I allow myself to be of service. True, I've experienced a growing awareness of my gifts over my lifetime; with some of the unusual life experiences I've had, it would have been hard not to. I have learned about my gifts and about the whole experience of spiritual healing mainly by trial and error, as well as through the help of some great teachers along the way. I feel a great deal of gratitude for Sister Sara, Father Guzman, Bob, and Don, as well as all the individuals whom I have shared healing sessions with.

I deeply believe the Absolute will always provide the opportunities and the teachers, as I am ready for them. I have come to be open to any situation. It was going to see Don for some psychotherapy regarding life-changing issues that first brought us together and also provided the kick in the rear I needed to start practicing as a full time spiritual healer. I am thankful now that I was open to that personal healing opportunity.

My collaboration with Bob happened in a similar fashion in that he came to me for healing and, over the time of working with him, I learned of his gifts. We were able to form a working relationship for a time. He was helpful and supportive, validating my gifts and the authenticity of what I was, in fact, already seeing and experiencing. This was all part of an effort that provided a great deal of education for my soul as well as for my personality. Bob also received gifts for the education of his soul. It is always through working together that we uncover our gifts and receive the necessary lessons. These experiences provide the platforms that educate our souls.

I have been most fortunate to experience and work with a variety of healing modalities. Teachers were brought to me, and I to them, often out of a physical need of some sort. A stiff neck, joint problems, the everyday aches and pains of life, have brought me into contact with physicians, chiropractors, physical therapists, massage therapists, acupuncturists, and psychotherapists. As I conversed with these practitioners, we eventually came around to a discussion of what I did for a living. Their curiosity always led us to some type of work together, perhaps on a certain client or patient. This was always done with full disclosure and consent, always honoring the free will of those involved.

I began to learn firsthand how spiritual healing can be used in conjunction with other modalities. Once again, the teachers and the opportunities were provided, as I was able to learn from them. As it always is with the Absolute, learning and healing occur for each person involved in the particular way he or she needs to receive the lesson. This is true whether or not we like the outcome of the interaction; we learn, grow and search. I readily admit that I will not be the solution for many of my collaborators; sometimes they will provide the solution I ed.   In writing this book and working with clients, I receive information and lessons from my Guides. Amazingly, what I have been taught experientially shows up in the research my friends and I did for the writing of this book. For millennia, other people have experienced the same lessons I have experienced, either by outright education or experientially, during their personal "mystic" journeys. It is reassuring to have this type of confirmation. After all, I'm only human, and I appreciate the back-up. This also demonstrates that what I do is a skilled procedure, which has been around for thousands of years. This is not New Age or new information; rather it is a possible new way of looking at total wellness through the eyes of a spiritual healer/ medium.

I can't stress enough how important it is for all of us to maintain an ethical, full and open, unending view of this dynamic. Spiritual healing must always be approached in innocence and without ego, not presuming to know, but only willing to be shown. All of the renowned seers throughout history have had to be egoless in their spiritual walk.

Ethics are a vital part of true spiritual healing. I am a healer, but I am human, and by definition I have ego. I must be aware of this at all times and constantly challenge myself to find my ego and make sure it is out of the way, for the good of my clients. It is a challenge I deal with all the time. I stay out of the way by making sure I know nothing of the individual's mental or physical health when I meet with them the first time.

Certain basic beliefs which I hold sacred, help me in my process. They include the sanctity of the body/soul union and the knowledge that anything of the divine comes through the Holy Spirit and never interrupts spiritual free will. There is no seduction, no control. When I'm finished with a session, I have no way of knowing how important or big the client's healing is going to be. Are they going to incorporate it or not, and if so, to what extent? Are they going to think the experience was good or useless? I let go of the interaction. In fact I get what friends and clients call "spiritual amnesia." I do not remember from one session to another, nor do I want to. My brain is too finite for other people's details. This is the reason the sessions sometimes need to be processed with a therapist who is familiar with and can work with Eternal Psychology™. The therapist can help the clients "connect the dots" of their healing sessions with me in a holistic way.

I want to tell you a story about a lady who performed a specific type of massage therapy. She was good at it, very intuitive, but not happy. Her allergies flared up and she got sore arms and shoulders, forcing her to move clients around to give her time to heal. I went to her because I needed some neck work. My Guides approved of the individual for some reason that I did not understand, as I already had a massage therapist to do the work. When I eventually told the therapist what I did for a living, she was very interested as she had many ailments herself.

She in turn came to me for a healing session. I was shown she had father issues that prevented her from fully committing to the practice of massage therapy and kept her away from the full development of her intuition. She had been to several therapists to help her, so she understood her issues well. She had an overwhelming desire to be of service to the divine so she could be more effective at whatever job she did. We exchanged sessions for a while. I got great benefit, but the amazing thing to me was the awakening of *her* gifts as she processed the points brought up in her healing sessions.

The therapist's clientele increased, as did her ability to help them. Her ability to see and feel her clients' needs opened. I made myself available for her to discuss this new ability to see and feel until she became comfortable with the gifts. Having someone to talk to about these events made it possible for her to use her gifts for the benefit of others. In the process, her arms, shoulder and allergies got better and she found joy in her life. She did not search for it; the joy just happened

My dream has always been to form a center for the purpose of supporting healers of all types in the innocent awakening of their personal discernment and gifts. This will be a foundation for the growth of all spiritual gifts as well as the education of the soul and connection to the Absolute. It is my purpose to create an environment within which people can begin to achieve this growth, learning to trust their own discernment within a safe place where their birthrights will naturally unfold. I believe that, in order for us to progress spiritually, it is crucial that we learn to be spiritually responsible through safely awakening our gifts in a spiritually ethical environment. This will take a great effort that I cannot do alone, so I constantly ask for guidance.

Those of you who have experienced one or more of the spiritual gifts I have described may be a little confused or even afraid of what is happening to you. Don't be; you are very fortunate. You have been given a gift that, if encouraged to grow in safety, will benefit you and humankind in many ways. The Absolute is alive and well, and spiritual healing is meant to be an integral part of our lives. If you have the gift, think of the good you can do for your brothers and sisters.

I hope I have given you at least an introduction to the world of spiritual healing and that you now realize it is not magical, threatening or weird. It is nothing more than a natural use of our intrinsic abilities and, as such, should be considered no stranger than thinking, breathing or eating, though it does require us to think beyond our current view of the world and how it works. In order to answer questions like "What is the meaning of life?" and "Why am I here?" we must challenge ourselves to go beyond the five senses, develop ego into a beneficial tool, and move past the tightly held beliefs that have slowed our spiritual growth.

It is my hope all who read this book have in some way been moved forward on their own spiritual path, and, as my colleague Don and others say, "allowed for the possibilities" of spirit. Perhaps you have new questions or a different way of considering spiritual experiences. Whatever your journey, I wish you well.

Glossary

Absolute: the life of the universe, the knowledge and thoughts that connect us all and connect all of our souls; the divine source, the foundation for the finite, and the basis of the infinite; the heart of spiritual healing; the reason for all life

Angel: a guide or messenger that has never been, and can never be, in physical form; an energetic being with no specific form

Aura: a sort of rainbow of light energy surrounding a living or non living being, symptomatic of the energy of that molecular structure or life form; the energy generated by the entire life force of each individual, thing or animal

Chakra system: the windows on our learning system or the points of contact between the etheric and physical bodies and the noetic system; consists of seven main chakras throughout the physical body but extending beyond, commonly referred to as the upper and lower chakras

Channeling: allowing an energy source to interrupt the sacred body-soul union and thereby enter one's body and control speech and actions

Christ Energy: (Logos) the energy from the Absolute that Jesus demonstrated throughout his life; the compassion and love that Jesus experienced in his physical life to provide us access to the energy of the Absolute

Elemental Energy: energy and mass created by our thoughts and the thoughts of animals, generating spiritual static; incidental energy; the energy of physical life and intent

Elementals: energy projected when we think a thought; incidental energy

EMDR: Eye Movement Desensitization and Reprocessing, a tool of psychotherapists

Eternal Psychology™: a multidimensional healing experience based on the collaboration of spiritual healing with psychotherapy and contributing to healing of the eternal soul

Etheric Body: the energetic presence that conducts electrical signals to the brain; the reflection of the physical body; the sum total of our life force and the source of our intuition; attaches the physical to the spiritual

Etheric Healing: Complete healing: spiritual, psychological, emotional and physical

Etheric membrane: the energy field that holds us all (physical, psychic and noetic) together

Etheric System: our complete existence, in all its forms, including the physical body, psychic body, noetic body and etheric membrane; allows us to experience non-physical aspects of existence while maintaining our individual energetic boundaries; includes the etheric body and the etheric membranes surrounding each of the bodies

Gift of command: the gift or ability to directly influence an individual's energy for healing, by direct intervention of Spirit, rather than working through prayer or petition (for example, identifying and then, with the client's free will consent, commanding negative energy to leave)

Grist: (Introject) strife; the inherent dissatisfaction that keeps each of us searching even when we have found "all the answers"

Guide: (possibly an angel) an energetic being with no specific form; an interpreter to the world of Spirit; your Master Guide is always with you and is reflected in your personality; (if the guide has existed in the physical world before, it is not an angel)

Introject: a learning tool to promote the evolution of the species; the inner, negative, parental voice within a child that reinforces fear-based beliefs unconsciously incorporated into one's personality; an inner voice preying on a person's sense of safety and ability to be loved; a self-generated, energetic, internal defense elemental, but subject to our spiritual free will

Kundalini: cord that connects the chakras so that the Absolute can nourish, replenish and cleanse us physically and spiritually; also called the etheric cord

Lifespan Integration (LI): a therapy introduced in 2002 by Peggy Pace to treat adults who suffered abuse or neglect in childhood. The client is guided to find a memory connected to the current problem and spontaneously generate a sequence of scenes that resolve the memory and gradually bring it to "healing" in the current phase of life

Meridians: Channels of physical energy flowing through the body

Noetic body: the "body of thoughts," the sum total of all of our learning through the emotions, thoughts and occurrences experienced by the physical body in this life, consisting of the inner chakra, the physical chakra and the spiritual chakra

Noetic system: a combination of the psychic and noetic bodies, able to extend into non-physical realms; continues on after the physical body dies

Paradigm: mental model or mind set by which we perceive and understand the world

Predatory energy: energy cut off from its divine source; "negative" energy that desires to be in and control a physical body in an effort to reunite with its divine source

Reiki: natural healing based upon "universal life force" energy; the physical manipulation of molecular energy

Sacred energy: intimate energy, one's "energetic fingerprints," the fund of knowledge that is "you" on all levels of existence; exists immortally with one's spirit; one's part of divinity

Soma: Life force of both the body and the soul

Soul progression: the fund of experience and knowledge your soul has gained since your creation; spiritual growth needed to access the fund of knowledge that existed before this life

Spirit: the working hand of divine perfection, the energy of everything

Spiritual free will: a direct, intrinsic, uninfluenced connection with our own soul, manifested in the connection between the physical and the spiritual, the body-soul union

Spiritual healer: one who chooses to be used as a tool of Spirit, within the boundaries of free will, to change the physical, mental and spiritual aspects of life; the catalyst that joins the healing theories of human experience with the education of the soul for full involvement with the Absolute by accessing the fund of knowledge that existed before the present lifetime

Spiritual healing: a quiet knowing that fills our lives with peace and the understanding of our true purpose; the education of the soul, which brings us closer to that which we call divine; a non-denominational, direct experience of the Absolute

Spiritual "homework": continued healing work sometimes with a psychotherapist to change the behaviors that caused or were created by the original physical or emotional disorder

Stigmata: the marks that can manifest on the physical body caused by the resistance, due to lack of knowledge, of the personality to be an instrument of the divine; often interpreted as the manifestations of the wounds suffered by Christ during the crucifixion

INDEX

About the Author: Eric Thorton

     Eric Thorton grew up in Washington State and attended an accelerated three-year Catholic high school, graduating on the honor roll. He then struggled for two years at the university where his undiagnosed dyslexia took its toll. Despite reading and writing difficulties, Eric discovered early on that he had excellent mechanical abilities. By age ten he was the neighborhood repairman. When he was twelve he remodeled his mother's kitchen. Between the ages of eighteen and twenty he managed a specimen tree farm for relatives. All along, though, he was experiencing unusual phenomena that he now knows were unique to him.

     At the age of twenty-nine Eric was married to the love of his life and was soon the happy father of two boys and a girl. After seventeen years of marriage, he claims his partner and their children as his grounding, his reason to live. "They have taught me so much about the circle of life and the joys of being a good parent and partner."

     Eric's mechanical brilliance eventually allowed him to start a handyman/remodel business that he would successfully maintain and enjoy for twenty years. While studying for an inspector's license and remodeling old homes, Eric founded his own home inspection firm. A few years later, when his dyslexia again precluded his successful test-taking, Eric recognized his true calling and saw that it had little to do with building or inspecting structures. Working like a human magnetic resonance imaging (MRI) machine, Eric sees into the human body. After viewing the patient's elemental energy, much as a psychic might do, he is led by the patient's spirit guide to that individual's sacred energy, the part as unique as a person's fingerprints. He is shown past experiences pertinent to the healing process and sometimes is used as a medium to bridge the gap to an important ancestor. He feels privileged to be part of such a wonderful process.

website:www.ericthorton.com

Printed in the United States
127597LV00004BA/2/P

9 780615 220994